AF291171

THE SPIRIT OF

MERCEDES

50 REASONS WHY WE LOVE THEM

FROM +60°C
MAYBACH
SL

THE SPIRIT OF

MERCEDES

50 REASONS WHY WE LOVE THEM

Vaughan Grylls

BATSFORD

CONTENTS

INTRODUCTION

The Spirit of Mercedes

Mercedes-Benz, the oldest and most famous maker of motorcars in the world, can trace its roots all the way back to 1885. Karl Benz at his small factory, Benz & Cie at Waldhofstraße 24 in Mannheim, Germany, was making coal-gas-driven four-stroke internal combustion engines, which were patented in 1877 by their inventor, Nikolaus Otto. Karl had improved what was known as the Otto Cycle engine to power machinery in workshops. In 1885 he thought of placing one into a three-wheeled chassis, and so in January 1886 he patented his confection as the Benz Patent-Motorwagen. Thus was the first motorcar born. Something must have been in the air because simultaneously just 65 miles (105km) away in the garden shed of Gottlieb Daimler's villa at Taubenheimstraße 13, Bad Cannstatt, just outside Stuttgart, Daimler and his friend, Wilhelm Maybach, took a horse-drawn carriage and dispensed with the horse and fitted a high-speed internal combustion engine of their own design. Thus was the first motorcar also born.

Above: The 1886 Daimler Motor Carriage - the world's first 'proper' car - wheels on all four corners.
Opposite: A vintage advertisement for the 1885 Benz Patent-Motorwagen.

Today it seems strange that given they were geographically close, Benz had no idea what Daimler and Maybach were up to and vice-versa, but this was a time before regular scientific journals or professional networks. Also there were the geographical and political divisions to consider. We have to remember that Germany only became one country in 1871.

In 1886, Otto lost his patent because a French engineer, Alphonse Beau de Rochas, had already described the four-stroke cycle in a theoretical patent in 1862. Otto's only consolation was that the Otto Cycle name stuck, but the loss of his patent meant that Benz, Daimler and Maybach could, from now on, develop and commercialize the first automobiles legally.

In 1901, Daimler-Motoren-Gesellschaft (DMG) as they were then called, made a 35 horsepower car. They named it after the daughter of a wealthy supporter of DMG, Emil Jellinek. From then on, a given name for a girl would be thought of firstly as the name of the most famous of car marques.

Although it first saw the light of day in 1909, representing land, sea and air, by 1926 the iconic three-pointed star was surrounded by laurel leaves. This recognised the merger of Benz & Cie with DMG that year to create Daimler-Benz. Now the three points could also be said to symbolise Benz, Daimler and Maybach.

A force it certainly was, epitomized in 1930 by the introduction of the Mercedes 770 or Großer Mercedes, a huge, luxury, jaw-dropping automobile. Built first as the WO7 and improved from 1938–43 as the W150 with a 7.7 litre straight-eight supercharged engine, it would become the wheels of choice for many of those in power, from the Japanese Emperor, Hirohito, to the Chancellor of Germany, Adolf Hitler.

During World War II, Daimler-Benz made trucks, armoured cars and aircraft engines for the German war effort. They used over 40,000 concentration camp prisoners, forced labourers and prisoners of war. After the war, the company acknowledged its role but it wasn't until 1988 that it apologized. A decade later, Daimler-Benz contributed 12 million Deutsche Marks to a compensation fund for former forced labourers.

Mercedes' reputation would recover, helped mostly by the success of the 170, a 1.7 litre car, introduced in 1931. Here was a car for the

better-heeled middle class. It was made in one form or another until 1955.

It would be difficult to imagine a Mercedes more iconic than the 300 SL coupé with its gullwing doors. Inspired by the W194 race car which had dominated the 1952 24-hour Le Mans, it wowed the 1954 New York Auto Show. This was the car for the stars. Today any 300 SL, whether a gullwing coupé or a convertible roadster is perhaps the most valuable classic to own.

Yet Mercedes, who had dominated racing in the early 1950s, withdrew from international motorsport following a horrible crash at the 1955 Le Mans, when a formidable 300 SLR *Uhlemhaut Coupé* left the track and careered into the crowd, killing its driver, Pierre Levegh, 83 spectators and injuring over 180. The company did the honourable thing and

Above left: An illustrated french advert for the 170 S. Above right: Mercedes-Benz 300 SL Coupe, Gullwing, in the Mercedes-Benz Museum.

withdrew from racing for more than 30 years. This, the worst crash in motor racing history, would lead to major changes in circuit design and crowd protection.

The 1960s saw the introduction of the 600 limousine, beloved of the Pope and the powerful. Made with bullet-proof build quality (and you could order one actually bullet-proof), sufficient time had passed for it not to revive memories of the tainted pre-war 700.

But the car of 1960s memory, certainly my own, has to be the 230, 250 and 280 SL sports tourers with their stunning removable hard-top – the pagoda roof. Designed by Paul Bracq, its slim elegance was

Above: The German team's Mercedes-Benz 300 SL during the 24 Le Mans race.
Below: A technical blueprint of a Mercedes-Benz 600 limousine from the 1960s.

a head-turner as it still is. The film director Stanley Donen used his own 230 SL for his 1966 spy thriller *Arabesque* with Sophia Loren or Gregory Peck at the wheel. The following year, he used his car again when he directed *Two for the Road* with Audrey Hepburn or Albert Finney now at the wheel. I love it.

1972 saw the introduction of the first S-Class. Here was a top-of-the-range luxury car, designed and built like no other. The W126 S-Class (1979–1991) would be regarded, and indeed envied by other manufacturers, as the epitome of engineering excellence, placing Mercedes as the maker of the best car in the world.

The S would also set the standard for all other classes of Mercedes. A glamorous two-seater SL, a respectable C- or E-Class family sedan, a sophisticated cabriolet or an off-road, go anywhere G-class, from the taxi-driver's 190 D to the majestic S, any Mercedes, especially those from the 1980s to the early 1990s, was guaranteed to be hewn from granite.

Except that created a challenge. Why should the world's taxi operators

Above left: A still of
Audrey Hepburn in a
Mercedes-Benz from
Two for the Road.
Above right: A still
of Sophia Loren and
Gregory Peck in a 230
SL, from *Arabesque*.

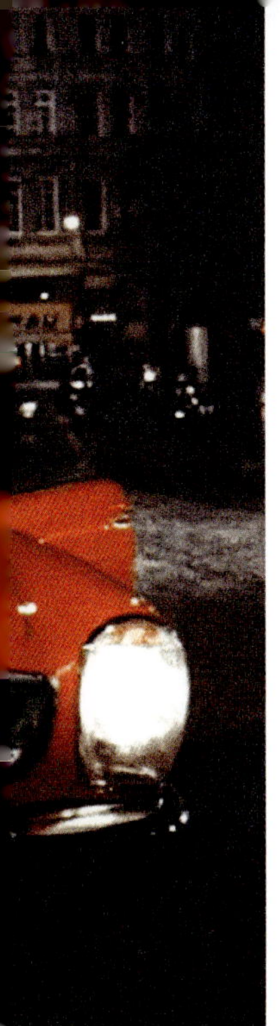

Above: A driver waits
with his Mercedes-Benz.
Below: Mercedes 190 E
as a taxi in Georgia.

spend money regularly replacing their fleets of 190 Ds? The ones they had would go on forever.

There was another, more serious challenge to consider. Mercedes may have been able to charge more for their cars than their premium competitors, Audi, BMW, Saab and Volvo. But not too much more, otherwise they could lose market share. In the crucial American market, BMW were overtaking Mercedes in sales with cars that were cheaper to make, comparably reliable, more exciting to drive, younger at heart and yet still thoroughly German. And BMW's profit margins were higher. Even Saab, a minnow of a company next to the others, was nibbling

away at Mercedes sales with its cool 900 Turbo and even cooler convertible. What to do?

The change took place on the model that had set the standard for Mercedes build quality, the over-engineered S-Class. The W140 version, built from 1991–1998 was now simply too expensive to sell at a price which could compete with BMW's 7 Series or Audi's A8. And now Toyota had joined the fray with its incredibly reliable Lexus LS400.

Mercedes answered with its W220 S-Class, introduced in 1998. While still a brilliantly performing car, lighter and more aerodynamically efficient than its predecessor, that definitive hewn feeling had gone for good. This car was of noticeably reduced build quality. The shift toward balancing luxury with cost efficiency was to be rolled out across all Mercedes' cars – the E, C, A, M, CLK and SL, with the possible exception of the G-Wagon. This deliberate decline in ruggedness hurt Mercedes' reputation, particularly in North America, where reliability and body strength were far more important factors when buying a car than in Europe.

Yet by increasing their profit margin, Mercedes weathered the inevitable storm of competition. But then they took a misstep. In 1998,

to gain a stronger foothold in North America, Daimler-Benz paid $36 billion for Chrysler. The rebranded DaimlerChrysler proved to be a huge mistake. There were cultural clashes, Chrysler was in poorer shape than Mercedes had been led to believe, and even worse, Chrysler's idea of cost-cutting went far beyond that which Mercedes had already implemented. In 2007 Mercedes grasped the nettle. Chrysler was sold to Cerberus Capital Management for a paltry $7.4 billion. It was a painful yet wise decision.

As for the European market, Mercedes had taken an even stranger decision in 1994 when they sealed a joint venture with Swatch, the Swiss watchmaker, to produce a small car called the Smart (an amalgam of sorts of Swatch, Mercedes and Art). The first model was launched in 1998 but Swatch pulled out completely by 2006, and in 2019 sold Smart as a joint venture to Geely in China. The unfortunately named brand was moved in its entirety to Geely. At least this attempt to take on the BMW Mini, the Fiat 500 or the Toyota iQ had not been badged a Mercedes.

Yet it wouldn't all be plain sailing after these Chrysler and Smart missteps. In 2015 the Dieselgate scandal broke. Volkswagen admitted

that they had falsified emission results during lab testing to make their cars appear compliant with US and European standards. Volkswagen executives were arrested and charged and Volkswagen ended up paying out over $35 billion in fines, legal costs and vehicle buy backs. It was a mighty fall for Germany's mightiest company.

The spotlight now fell on BMW and Mercedes. Unlike Volkswagen, both denied deliberate cheating. Unfortunately defeat devices were found on some Mercedes models but no 'official' ones on BMWs. Mercedes owned up and were fined $3 billion while BMW who didn't own up, got away with €380 million.

In 1998 Volkswagen acquired the Rolls-Royce and Bentley brands. A tussle followed between Volkswagen and BMW, who already supplied engines to Rolls-Royce and also held the rights to the RR name and logo. Eventually a gentlemanly carve-up was agreed. Volkswagen would keep the Bentley brand, BMW the Rolls-Royce.

What did this carve-up have to do with Mercedes? Quite a lot. Mercedes feared that their German rivals would now aim at upstaging them with these prestige brands. They cast around for an equivalent

and settled on a marque they already owned – Maybach, named for one of the original founders of the company. In 2002, Mercedes launched the Maybach 57 and 62 models. They were at least as good as BMW's Rolls-Royces and Volkswagen's Bentleys. Probably better.

But there was a problem. Maybachs had been built in Friedrichshafen on Lake Constance from 1921, with the last built in 1941 and a few after the war. So it wasn't very surprising that nobody, other than car buffs, had ever heard of Maybach.

Sales were so dire that in 2012 Mercedes ditched Maybach as a standalone brand, reintroducing it in 2014 as the Mercedes-Maybach, a luxury-plus version of their top models.

Looking back we may ask why the Maybach detour had been embarked on. After all, Mercedes-Benz itself was the most famous car brand in the world.

Perhaps the Maybach thing came out of the confidence-knocking the company had received with their ill-fated Chrysler and Smart ventures. But hindsight is, of course, a fine thing.

Mercedes' greatest contemporary achievement has been with

their AMG models. A small company founded in 1967, specializing in tuning Mercedes for motorsport, AMG is an abbreviation of the founders' names, Hans Aufrecht and Erhard Melcher while the G is from Großaspach, Hans' hometown.

AMG had become very successful with models such as the SEL 6.8 AMG at the 24 Hours of Spa in 1971 and the 1986 AMG Hammer, a souped-up E-Class with a V8 engine. In 1990, Mercedes allowed AMG to sell performance models through their own dealerships. This brilliant move was followed by part ownership, with full ownership of AMG by Mercedes in 2005. In doing so, Mercedes took the high-performance fight to BMW's M and Audi's RS divisions. Today Mercedes-AMG is committed to full electrification with its AMG.EA platform. An exciting future awaits.

Mercedes has a history of automobile design and production like no other. Ups and downs were inevitable given that the company has been going longer than any other car manufacturer. Yet that lustrous logo still

manages to hold prime place in the world of automobiles, despite stiff opposition from companies with vaster resources, such as Volkswagen with its Audi and Toyota its Lexus.

Today, in the race for an all-electric line-up, legacy-brand manufacturers, and even Tesla, are facing fierce competition from new Chinese brands now flooding the market in eye-watering volume. In China new models can be developed in an astonishing 12 months. Luckily for the luxury segment Mercedes sells into, this fight is currently focused at the other end of the market. Yet as day follows night, luxury Chinese cars are coming.

Mercedes has, in the long run, seen off competition for the Car Crown before, simply because it is the legacy brand with a pedigree and spirit like no other.

So here are 50 reasons why we love Mercedes-Benz, starting with my Dream-On Two Dozen – 12 from before WWII and 12 after. These are the Mercedes I'd really like to test-drive, given the chance – and you may too!

Opposite: A 2024 electric Mercedes AMG EQE 53.
Above: The iconic logo.

01

1901 MERCEDES 35 PS

I'm not starting with that 1886 first motorwagen, simply because it was a prototype, and anyway it would be impossible to teach me how to drive it. No, I'd like to get behind the wheel of a car I could have bought at the time. So now we are in 1901, when the first commercially available Mercedes is a 35 PS.

It has a 5.9 litre four-pot engine, delivering 35 horsepower, at a time when that is the only power measure going. It has a 4-speed gearbox, a low-slung, pressed-steel frame, a long wheel-base, a honeycomb radiator and an engine you could recognize as one, even today. It has made all those adapted horse-drawn carriages obsolete. Who wouldn't love to get behind the wheel of a Mercedes 35 PS, the first real car?

The 35 PS was commissioned by Emil Jellinek, a successful Austrian businessman based in Nice. Emil said to Daimler-Motoren-Gesellschaft that he would agree to becoming the sole agent for their car throughout the Austrian Empire, France and the United States as long as it was named after his daughter.

So it would come to pass that Daimler-Motoren-Gesellschaft made the car, while Emil's daughter's name made the company a byword for innovation and quality.

The passenger in the front seat of this 35 PS is Mrs de Rothschild, wife of the owner of the car's coachbuilder, J. Rothschild et Fils of Paris. Struggling at the wheel is Mrs de Gast, – or maybe de Gust, given the conditions.

Various angles of the
1910 Mercedes 37/90
HP: being driven (above
and below right) and the
engine (below left).

02

1910 MERCEDES 37/90 HP

By 1910, Germany had enjoyed a half-century reputation for building the world's finest grand pianos such as those manufactured by Bechstein, Blüthner and Steinway. All were beautifully fashioned from the best materials — and loud when the occasion demanded it.

This Mercedes 37/90 very much followed that German tradition. Before World War I, it was the fastest and most powerful road car in the world, capable of 70mph (113kph) thanks to a massive 9.5 litre engine, designed by Paul Daimler, which in 1913 was increased to 9.8 litres for the 38/100.

As with German pianos, these cars set the scene for Mercedes' legendary reputation for over-engineering.

Assuming you were rich enough to buy one, you could order anything from an open tourer to a formal landaulette with exquisite and exclusive coachwork by companies such as J. Rothschild et Fils, Erdmann & Rossi or Vanvooren. Unsurprisingly, owners included such luminaries as Tsar Ferdinand of Bulgaria.

Although the 37/90 and 38/100 were not designed for racing, their outstanding abilities in everything from hill-climbs to long-distance trials to point-to-point speed trials was soon made obvious. Intrepid, to say the least.

03

1914 MERCEDES
GRAND PRIX RACE CAR

The 1914 Mercedes Grand Prix was the finest racing car of its type, thanks to its mechanical toughness and sophisticated design, winning race after race, before war intervened. It had a 4.5 litre inline 4-cylinder engine producing 106hp and a 3-speed gearbox, a rarity at the time.

Here it is driven by Christian Lautenschlager in Lyon at the French Grand Prix in 1914, the very last international car race before war broke out. This was a 467 mile (752km) race over rough, unpaved roads and in searing heat.

Mercedes entered five cars, winning first, second and third place thanks to expert driving, German engineering, a low centre of gravity and excellent road-holding — all much to the dismay of the French.

Here is a century-old example at the Goodwood Festival of Speed in 2014. Imagine getting behind the wheel of this beauty.

Above: The Mercedes that Lautenschlager won the 1914 Grand Prix in.
Below: A Mercedes GP racer 100 years later at Goodwood Festival of Speed, 2014.

04

1914–18 AND 1921 BENZ 10/30 PS

Announced in 1912 by Benz & Cie, the 10/30 PS was manufactured, albeit in heavily reduced numbers, throughout World War I.

Production ceased completely in 1918 but the car was reintroduced three years later at a time when Germany was grappling with economic hardship, terrible inflation and social upheaval.

Understandably, glamour and racing glory were now out and a cautious, sensible approach in. Here was the car for doctors, lawyers and headmasters – quiet, dignified middle-class styling for those who had survived the devastating war and now craved stability over speed.

The 10/30 had a 4-cylinder, 2.6 litre engine and coachwork was typically a four-door sedan, although you could go off-piste and order an open-topped tourer or phaeton. Not many did.

Although never a performance car in any form, the 10/30 PS's smooth running, low maintenance and reliability would play a crucial role in ensuring the survival of not just Daimler-Benz but the German motor industry itself. So I do think that being offered the chance to drive one would be rather special.

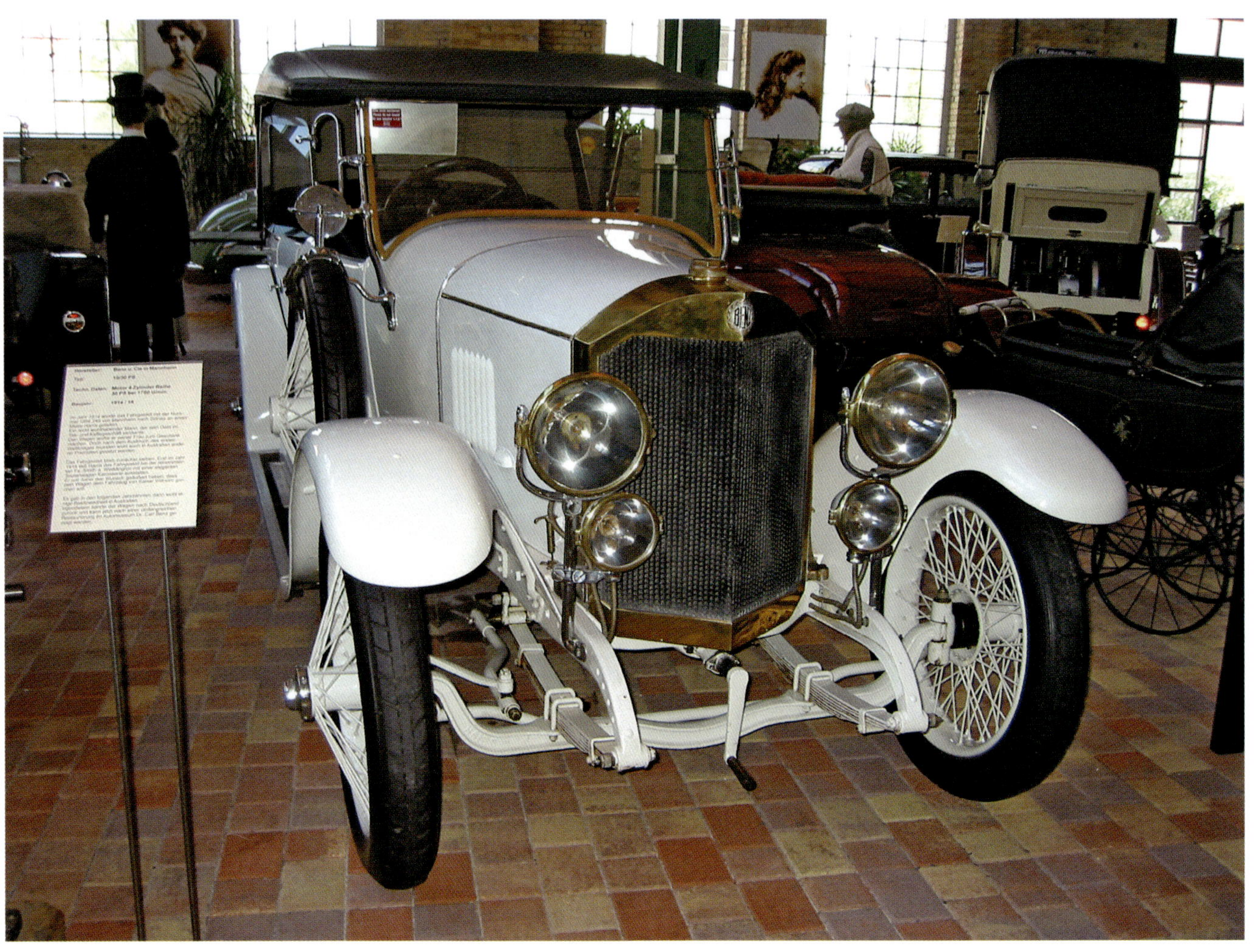

Two classic Benz 10/30
PS cars on display.

05

1926 MERCEDES-BENZ 24/100/140 PS TYP K

After the 1926 merger, the 24/100/140 PS Typ K (designated as the 24/110/160 from 1929), designed by Ferdinand Porsche, was the first major statement from the newly formed company of Daimler-Benz.

By the mid-1920s, when the Jazz Age began to displace the horrific memories of the Great War, Mercedes saw an opportunity. The world's rich, including those in Germany who had somehow managed to hang on to, or make money since the war's end, were the target.

The Typ K (for *kurz*, meaning shortened) was Mercedes' earlier 24/100/140 PS model from 1924, with a 6.2 litre supercharged 6-cylinder engine, fitted onto a, you've guessed it, shortened chassis. This gave the car 140 horsepower, a top speed approaching 90mph (145kph) and phenomenal acceleration when the Roots blower was brought into play. This car would bring Mercedes back to their pre-war position of winning race after race.

The Typ K had also taken the luxury fight to bespoke manufacturers such as Hispano-Suiza and Rolls-Royce. Mega luxury with mega speed – what's not to like? The mega-rich were thrilled, especially when development continued with ever more powerful versions of the Typ K, such as the 24/110/160 which was introduced in 1929.

They still are, for surviving examples are among the most sought after inter-war Mercedes.

Varying angles of a
running Mercedes-Benz
24/100/140 PS Typ K.

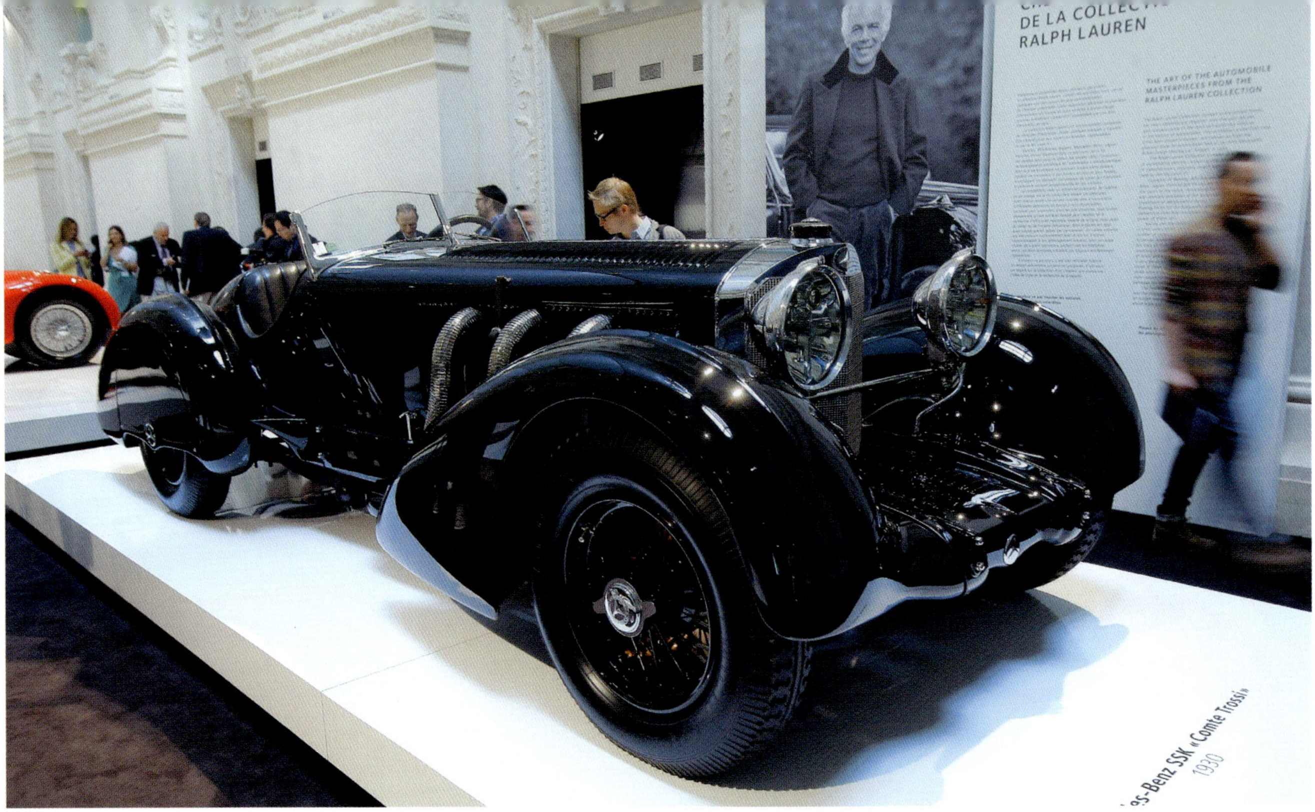

DE LA COLLECTION
RALPH LAUREN

THE ART OF THE AUTOMOBILE
MASTERPIECES FROM THE
RALPH LAUREN COLLECTION

...s-Benz SSK «Comte Trossi»
1930

06

1928 MERCEDES-BENZ SSK (SUPER SPORT KURZ)

The SSK was perhaps the most illustrious creation of Ferdinand Porsche's work with Mercedes and indeed one of the company's most famous pre-war models.

With its 7.1 litre engine and the supercharger engaged, the SSK could make 120mph (193kph) with around 225 horsepower. That rivalled aircraft engines of the time. Unsurprisingly this car would dominate motorsport throughout the late 1920s and early 1930s.

The SSK's racing prowess was spectacular, especially with Mercedes' Rudolf Caracciola at the wheel, where its sheer speed and thunderous mechanical presence made an intimidating sight on any course, particularly at the 1929 and 1930 Mille Miglia races, which he won outright.

The SSK was usually stripped down with minimal coachwork and an exposed side exhaust. In Mercedes tradition, form followed function as seen in this version at the Nürburgring in 1930.

Raw, brutal power may have been the name of the game, but that didn't mean you couldn't commission something bespoke from specialist coachbuilders such as Saoutchik or Corsica. The streamlined version was commissioned by Count Carlo Felice Trossi, an Italian aristocrat, playboy and formidable driver of Italian racing cars in the 1930s and 40s. Here it is prepared for racing and in action at Essex, Macsachusetts in 2002 and again in 2011 at the Ralph Lauren Collection in Paris. Today an SSK could fetch well north of $6 million.

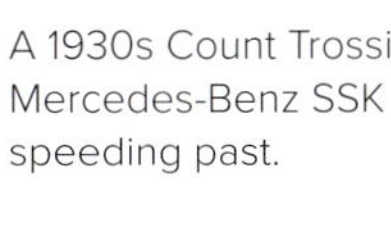
A 1930s Count Trossi
Mercedes-Benz SSK
speeding past.

07

1930 MERCEDES-BENZ NÜRBURG 460

Aimed at the top of the chauffeur market, then dominated by Cadillac, Packard and Rolls-Royce, this was Mercedes' first 8-cylinder car.

The Nürburg 460 had real presence. Powered by a 4.6 litre in-line engine specially designed to be super-quiet and easy to maintain, it had a top speed of 65mph (105kph), then considered quite enough for important passengers and a car weighing over two tons.

Here is the cabriolet version in 1929, complete with the Queen of the Netherlands in a black hat.

Would you rather play chauffeur or passenger before deciding whether you love this admittedly splendid Mercedes Nürburg 460 Cabriolet?

Freudenstadt

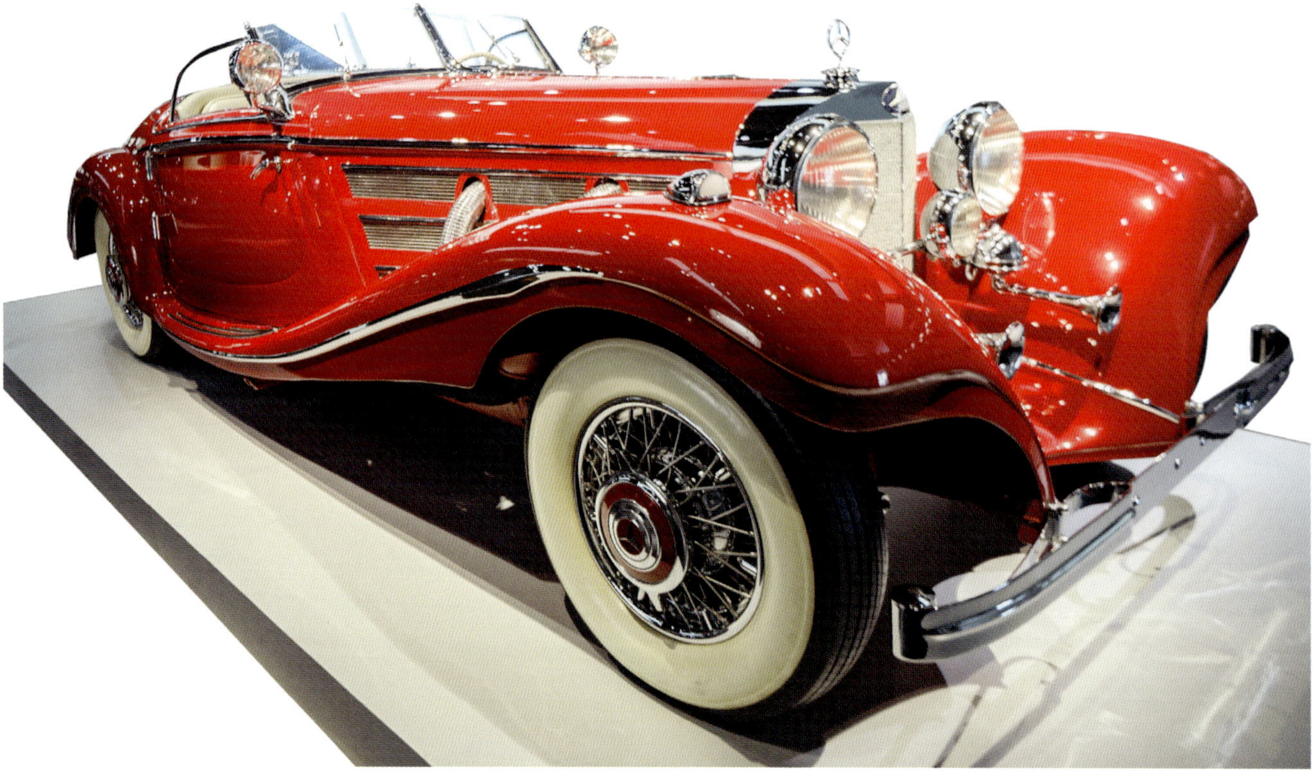

08

1934 MERCEDES-BENZ 500K SPECIAL ROADSTER

Should you crave a pre-war supercharged symbol of opulence, look no further than here.

Unveiled at the 1934 Berlin Motor Show, the 500K Special Roadster was designed by Friedrich Geiger, who after the war would go on to design the iconic 300 Gullwing and the first S-Class.

Many 500K punters wanted their own touches included, and Mercedes was happy to oblige at their bespoke vehicle construction facility, meaning you could have that *Sindelfingen* badge attached giving you additional discreet bragging rights.

This car may look like a two-seater but it's a four, because the back folds out to reveal a Dickey Seat, sometimes called the Mother-in-Law seat. In Agatha Christie's *Poirot* stories, that was often the first place to look for the suspect – or indeed the murder victim.

Why wouldn't you want to drive one?

09

1936 MERCEDES-BENZ 170 H

This may look an odd choice for my Dream-On Two Dozen. But when you come to think about it, why not? This car was one of the most daring departures in pre-war German automotive engineering because it was one of the earliest production cars in the world to place the engine behind the rear axle.

The H stands for *heckmotor*, or rear engine – a 1.7 litre driving the rear wheels. That meant a flat floor and no driveshaft tunnel. And the weight distribution gave excellent traction on the rough and rutted roads of rural Europe, as well as snow and ice.

Why did it fail? Well, Ferdinand Porsche's KdF-Wagen (Strength Through Joy Car), known as the Beetle or Bug post-war, enjoyed Hitler's backing. And the idea of a pint-size Mercedes for the masses was to most punters puzzling to say the least. Especially in America.

Yet the Mercedes 170 H was ahead of its time. Sadly, very few survive today which makes it a firm favourite for collectors of oddballs. And that's a good enough reason to take one for a spin.

10

1936 MERCEDES-BENZ TYPE 260 D

One more oddball.

Der Erste Personenwagen DIESEL. The first passenger automobile in series production with an oil burner for an engine. And this oddball did sell pretty well.

Launched at the Berlin Motor Show in 1936, the 260 D, was produced as a full-size sedan, with landaulette and cabriolet versions available. The engine was 2545cc OHV 4-cylinder instead of a 6-cylinder which had been discarded because there was too much vibration.

A full-size Mercedes-Benz 260 D Pullman (W138) sedan on display in the Mercedes-Benz Museum.

The 260 D may have been a slow car – top speed 59mph (95kph) – but it had low fuel costs and low maintenance. Many were sold as taxis. They were also rather good at towing things, as seen in this 1937 photo of a 260 D Cabriolet.

The fuel-injected diesel engine was such an advance that it is celebrated today as a work of art as well as science. Here is one proudly displayed in Moscow.

Would I like to drive an example of this extremely rare *clatterwagen* – that's if I could find one? You bet!

Above: A Mercedes-Benz 260 D post restoration at the Moscow Exhibition of Technical Antiques. Opposite: A 1937 Mercedes 260 D Cabriolet towing a caravan in the countryside.

IIA - 51117

11

1938 MERCEDES 540K AUTOBAHN KURIER

First unveiled at the 1936 Paris Motor Show, and also designed by Friedrich Geiger, the 540Ks (which were lighter than the 500Ks, which used the chassis design – a girder style – similar to the SSK) replaced the steel girders with lighter oval-section tubes, developed for the *Silver Arrows*, Mercedes' racing cars. The straight 8-cylinder engine was now 5.4 litres.

Three chassis variations were available, and if that wasn't enough, there was a wide choice of clothes – two- and four-seater cabriolets, a four-seater coupé and even a seven-seater limo complete with armoured side panels and glass.

Hermann Göring's car was similarly equipped, although being open-topped, he would have had to duck should he come under fire. Then there was the six-wheeled 540 G4, a birthday present from Adolf Hitler to General Franco, still on parade in 2022 at the swearing-in of King Felipe VI of Spain's Royal Guard.

Above: King Felipe VI
of Spain in the armoured
1939 Mercedes 540 G4.
Below: A colour-
restored image of
Hermann Göring's car.

Yet I think the most amazing-looking 540 was the *12 Autobahn Kurier*, designed for high-speed cruising on Germany's new autobahn network. Only a handful were made, but if I ever had the chance, this is the car I'd like to hammer down an autobahn. Dream on. Here are three of them at the 2021 Concours d'Elegance car show in Pebble Beach, California.

lot 007
1939 Mercedes-Benz
...Grosser Offener Tourer
$ 7,000,000
€ 5,745,215
£ 5,063,772
WorldwideAuctioneers.com
IA 148 461

12

1939 MERCEDES-BENZ 770K GROßER OFFENER TOURENWAGEN

If there is one Mercedes that projects absolute prestige more than any other, the 770K Großer (large, as if you hadn't guessed) is it. That's because it was designed for that singular purpose. For President Hindenburg, Emperor Hirohito, Pope Pius XI, Adolf Hitler, Benito Mussolini and Francisco Franco, a 770 Großer was the automobile of choice.

The Series I was introduced in 1930. The Series II ran from 1938 to 1944.

The Großer had a straight 8-cylinder engine of 7665cc. A Roots type supercharger was available which could project the beast to 99mph (160kph), should the occupant desire a quick escape. In fact a twin supercharger became available providing an even quicker escape of up to 118mph (190kph). This Großer, was 'liberated' by the US Army in 1945. It was used as an army staff car by the Americans and was thought to have belonged to Hermann Göring. But much later, when it was under restoration, it was established that this was the actual car that a triumphant Hitler had used for his victory parade through the streets of Berlin in 1940 in celebration of the capitulation of France.

The Großer, of course, had to make this list of Dream-Ons and indeed finish the pre-war section. But would I like to get behind the wheel of this particular car? Maybe not.

Opposite: Hitler's Mercedes up for auction in 2018.
Above: Hitler in his Mercedes 770 Großer.

13

1949 MERCEDES-BENZ
170 S CABRIOLET B

So … for my next Dream Dozen, let's go post-war and start with this looker.

Believe it or not this automobile was based on the pre-war 170V, a strong if stolid car.

Yet this was a swan – a luxurious, elegant post-war convertible, celebrating Mercedes' commitment to quality and craftsmanship, but designed and built at a challenging time.

This, Cabriolet B, the poshest in the 170 S series, offered a smooth ride, a power-folding soft top, wood trim, beautiful leather, and that Mercedes hallmark – a meticulous attention to detail throughout. It was a riposte to the devastation and austerity of post-war Europe, an unequivocal message that Mercedes-Benz was back in the luxury car business within just three years of the end of World War II.

Today, the 170 S Cabriolet B is a rare and sought-after classic, and although its 1.7 litre 52 horsepower four-pot engine made it no racehorse, I would just love to get behind the wheel of one.

A silver 1955 Mercedes
300 SL Coupé Gullwing
with red interior on
display.

14

1955 MERCEDES-BENZ 300 SL GULLWING

Few cars, if any, have ever made as bold an entrance, or left as lasting an impression, as the jaw-dropping 300 SL Gullwing (W198). Derived from the race-proven W194 of the early 1950s, the SL debuted at the 1954 New York Auto Show to instant acclaim. Its iconic upward-opening doors were no mere design flourish: they were of necessity, thanks to the car's innovative tubular spaceframe chassis (SL – *Super Leicht* or Super Light), leaving no room for conventional side-hinged doors. That would become the most recognizable visual signature in the history of the motorcar.

The engineering was by Rudolf Uhlenhaut and the body by Friedrich Geiger. It was born thanks to Max Hoffman, the official Mercedes importer in the US who, seeing what their W194 race cars were doing, said that if they built a road car version, he could sell 1000 of them in America. He was right.

With a 3.0 litre straight-six engine and Bosch mechanical fuel injection, a world first in a production car, a 300 SL could reach 160mph (258kph). And that made it the fastest road car of its day.

Everyone who was anyone in the 1950s – Clark Gable, Sophia Loren, Juan Fangio, to name just three – sat behind the wheel of one.

It was followed in 1957 by an open-topped version, the roadster.

Yet the Gullwing was not just a celeb trophy. It was a precision machine, capable of grand touring at speed with uncanny poise, even by today's standards. In fact, the 300 SL Gullwing is arguably the most famous car in the world today.

What did you say ... would I like to drive one?

A bright red Mercedes 300SL Roadster driving along a scenic route.

15

1955 MERCEDES-BENZ 300 SC COUPÉ

If grandeur is your thing, and just sometimes it's mine too, look no further than this hand-built grand tourer which combined pre-war dignified presence with an engine derived from the legendary 300 SL Gullwing. That meant that when called on, dignified presence could give way very quickly to undignified acceleration and roadholding at a standard previously unseen in such a stately coupé.

Only 200 coupés and cabriolets were ever built between 1955 and 1958, making it one of the rarest and most collectible Mercedes.

This was a statement of European refinement, from wood-trimmed dashboard to bespoke luggage compartment. I'll give the chauffeur time off and get behind the wheel myself.

Opposite: Different angles of a burgundy 300 SC Coupé.

16

1969 MERCEDES-BENZ 280 SL 'PAGODA'

When you think of a car for the 1960s, what springs to mind? An E-Type Jag? A Mini? For me it has to be the car featured in the 1967 movie, *Two For The Road*, starring Audrey Hepburn and Albert Finney. Here was Mercedes' most successful demonstration of elegance and glamour.

Designed by Paul Bracq with input from legendary designers, Bela Barényi (godfather of the VW Beetle) and the equally legendary Rudolf Uhlenhaut (who gave his name to the 300 SLR Coupé), these cars were built at Mercedes' famous Sindelfingen studio near Stuttgart. They boasted that iconic dished pagoda roof which was removable, assuming you were strong enough to do so unaided. It was better if you had a Mercedes hoist in your garage, which I hadn't, so it helped to be young.

This was the car in which to float around serenely, which I did, with the occasional London van driver shouting out of the window, 'Hey chief!

Opposite: My 280SL without its roof.
Above: An older picture of the car outside my gallery and with its roof.

Some of us have to get to work, you know!' And often ruder things. Well, wouldn't you? Just look at it.

The 230 SL was introduced in 1963 with a choice of manual or automatic gearboxes. Upgraded in 1966 as the 250 SL with such advances as rear disc brakes, the following year it was upgraded again as the 280 SL. That was the best of the bunch, with its muscular 2.8 litre straight six engine offering 168 horsepower. The 280 SL was made until 1971.

Although no full-blooded sports car, whether manual or automatic, the 230 SL and its two successors were a radical departure for Mercedes from its spartan forerunners, the 300 and 190. Instead these were for those lusting after a beautifully built sports tourer offering elegance and glamour as soon as they took the wheel.

Which is why my manual 280 SL was so dear to my heart, because I possessed neither.

A very shiny brown
Mercedes-Benz 450
SEL.

17

1975 MERCEDES-BENZ
450 SEL 6.9 LITRE

This flagship of the W116 range, called simply the 6.9 in North America, was launched at the Geneva Motor Show in 1974. This was the first car in the world to be fitted in 1978 with ABS, an electronic, all-wheel anti-lock braking system, developed by Bosch. It needed it, given it was one of the heaviest and certainly the fastest sedan in the world, with its huge V8 – 62mph (100kph) in 7.4 seconds and a top speed of 140mph (225kph) – still no slouch half a century later. If that wasn't enough, the car featured hydropneumatic self-levelling suspension.

Here was *the* super-sedan for heads of state and captains of industry, with, as you would expect, wall-to-wall restrained Teutonic opulence.

In 1976, the French movie director Claude Lelouch made an eight-minute artwork of his high-speed drive through Paris in the early hours of an August Sunday. His camera, slung below the car's front fender, so necessarily small and therefore not self-levelling, captured Lelouch charging through red lights, the wrong way up one-way streets and reaching maximum speed on the Avenue Foch, all while taking in a backdrop of famous Parisian landmarks.

450 SEL
508 BGS 77

Left: The DVD cover of Lelouch's *C'etait un Rendezvous*.
Opposite: The back of the shiny brown 450 SEL.

Lelouch filmed in one take, with the sound of his Ferrari 275GTB thundering away. The film finishes in Montmartre with Lelouch getting out of his Ferrari and throwing his arms around his girlfriend as the bells of Sacré-Coeur ring out against the sound of a beating heart. Well, this is Paris.

So how about the car that delivered such a lunatic drive? Ferrari performance combined with hydropneumatic, self-levelling suspension on Parisian cobbles? What's not to like? It would be fun to get behind that Ferrari's wheel.

Except such a car didn't exist. So I'll settle for the stunt car that actually delivered for the Ferrari.

18

1985 MERCEDES-BENZ 560 SEC

Could there ever have been a car built like a tank, but sexy with it? Yes there could – the 560 SEC, the top of the top of the range S-Class.

There really was no true competitor for those demanding in one place, prestige, reliability, build-quality, quiet, effortless performance and raciness as you could find in abundance in this massively over-engineered pillarless coupé. Eat your hearts out Audi, BMW and Jaguar.

The 500 (sold mostly into the European market) had a smaller engine, but the 560 with extra crash-safety additions (mandated by the US authorities) such as heavy-duty side bars in the doors and extra front and rear protection, required a bit more muscle up front to counter the added weight. So the 560 sold very well into the US market to those dreaming of smooth, high-speed, transcontinental non-stop drives – other than for fuel, given that you'd be visiting petrol stations quite often at 12mpg (19kpg). Of course most wouldn't be seen belting across America, but floating around neighbourhoods such as Beverly Hills and Westchester, New York.

As for those Europeans who wanted that extra muscle *and* the 560 badge but without that American extra weight – they could have one on special order. It wasn't necessary, of course, as for pure driveability these cars could really shift in any version. But in the 1980s, bling was king.

I'd like to try one out on a racetrack. Although, come to think of it, floating around Beverly Hills may be quite enough to savour a car built like no other.

A blue 1985 Mercedes 560 SEC parked outside a house in Beverly Hills.

J548 LRP

19

1991 MERCEDES-BENZ 500 SL (R129)

The R129 series of SLs were the true inheritors of how to do the Mercedes two-door sports tourer thing in style, last seen in the classic pagoda roof models of the 1960s. True, there was the one in between, the R107 and C107 which went on and on from 1971 until 1989. Yet, compared to the pagoda, it was buffalo front-heavy, although it was a magnificently built car and, whisper it, a much better driver than its elegant predecessor.

Over the life of the R129s, produced between 1988 and 2001, there were several engines on offer – straight 6, V8 and V12, ranging from a 280 SL up to a 600 SL. There was even a hooligan version, the 518hp SL73 AMG. This car could touch 200mph (322kph), thanks to its 7.3 litre V12. Only 50 were made. So you'd have better luck finding a unicorn than one of those today.

Yet it would be the 322 horsepower 500 SL with its 5 litre V8 that, like the pagoda roof models, somehow caught the public imagination.

Princess Diana and her
somewhat controversial
Mercedes 500 SL.

Some years ago, a 500 SL caught my imagination, not least because it had once belonged to King Hussein of Jordan, who apparently kept it in London for his private perambulations when in town. With the top down, he must have worn sunglasses.

I didn't buy it and, in fact, Princess Diana shouldn't have had hers either, judging by the hoo-hah she caused by being the first member of the Royal Family to buy a foreign car. Following a tabloid campaign, she returned it to the leasing company. Today, it is proudly displayed in the Mercedes Museum. Quite right too.

20

2002 MAYBACH

Doing an *AMGUC* I call it — *Ask My Grown-Up Children.* Here goes.

'Have you ever heard of the Hon. C.S. Rolls and Sir Henry Royce?'

'Of course, Dad.'

'Gottlieb Daimler and Karl Benz?'

'Er … Daimler Benz? … Mercedes?'

'Yep. What about Wilhelm Maybach?'

Three shaking heads.

Maybach was the brilliant technical director of Daimler (DMG). In the late-19th century he was called the 'King of Automobile Design'. In 1907 he founded his own company, after a spat with Paul Daimler, son and successor to Gottlieb. Wilhelm made a name for himself designing engines for Zeppelins which were powerful and reliable, yet lightweight.

After World War I, when military business had dried up, he started building his own luxury cars, at Friedrichshafen on scenic Bodensee, which we know as Lake Constance, and he branded them with his own name. They were as beautiful as the place in which they were made.

In 1929 Wilhelm died. Maybach cars then became something of a sideline because his son Karl, sniffing the air, decided that business should again be concentrated on military contracts, leading to the superb lightweight yet powerful engines for the feared Panther and Tiger tanks used in World War II. Yet the few Maybach cars built were still stunning.

A black and white photo of a 1930s Maybach DS8 Stromlinien.

Funnily enough, Wilhelm Maybach never owned a car himself. He preferred the tram. He sounds an eccentric genius, a fascinating man who made superb cars. But that is not enough reason to re-introduce a luxury car brand over 60 years later, just because BMW now owned the Rolls-Royce and VW the Bentley brands. After all, top-flight Mercedes cars were considered in the same class as Rolls and Bentley. Even the Pope thought so.

Maybach sales were a disaster. And that was a shame because the Maybach limousines were once again better designed and built than the competition.

Unfortunately those with oodles of money don't have to think logically all the time. They can afford not to. Which is why a lovely Range Rover with iffy reliability is much preferred over a lovely Lexus that is never back at the dealer. A worldwide brand is everything. Maybach wasn't.

You don't spy many Maybachs these days, so here is a brace of them in a fitting German setting.

Today, Mercedes use Maybach as a sub-title, and also Zeppelin, to identify the most luxurious versions of their cars such as the S-Class and the Mercedes-Maybach SL680 Monogram Series.

But I would like to test-drive the simply badged Maybach 57 or 62, named just for this remarkable man. And while in cosseting mode, why not get behind the wheel of that SL680?

The only thing is that, in the spirit of Herr Maybach himself, I wouldn't be interested in owning any of these brilliant cars. Which is a bit sad, but they are just not me. BTW, it's pronounced *My-bachh* – as if you didn't know already.

AMG
DRIVING PERFORMANCE
CLA

21

2017 MERCEDES-BENZ S63 AMG (C217)

Launched in 2013, this S-Class had five models available - Standard (W222), Long wheel-base (V222), Maybach (X222), Cabriolet (A217) and the Coupé (C217), shown here at the 2017 Frankfurt Motor Show. A Cabriolet can be seen in the background.

These cars may have appeared relatively restrained, but their power was brutal - true fists in velvet gloves.

This 4MATIC all-wheel drive S63 AMG, boasted – quietly of course – a 5.5 litre V8 producing 577 horsepower. Complete with diamond-stitched leather in which to settle your bottom at a regulated 155mph (250kph) and with more tech than you could shake a stick at, this car was an Annihilator of the Autobahn.

A silver Mercedes-Benz S63 AMG on display at the Frankfurt IAA Motor Show.

22

2021 MERCEDES-BENZ EQS 580 4MATIC

How do you square sensible electric motoring with S-Class luxury and dynamic performance? The answer is PDQ with BMW breathing down your neck. Mercedes scored a hit by launching their standard-setting EQS 580 in 2021, a full year before the B-word's i7. Hurrah!

   With 523 horsepower, 360 to 422 miles (580 to 680km) on one charge of 80 per cent in half an hour, it is impressive, even when you discount any manufacturer's quoted range and charge times – which we all do.

   This car has dual-electric motors, 0–62mph (0–100kph) in 4.3 seconds, adaptive air-suspension and a top speed of over 130mph (210kph). In short, here is a whisper-quiet luxury projectile.

The fully electric
Mercedes-Benz EQS
sedan.

23

2024 MERCEDES-AMG GT63 S E PERFORMANCE

If you like V8 muscle jolted by hybrid-system electrification to give blistering acceleration in a four-door coupé, here it is. The rear-mounted electric motor is F1-derived, giving an extra 200 horsepower on tap.

When it comes to brake horsepower in a four-door, this AMG with 831, socks it to BMW Group's MG Competition with its 625 and VW Group's Porsche Panamera Turbo S E-hybrid with its 690. This car, however, is discreet even in green, although mentioning that colour, it is no planet-saver. Green here simply means envy. Give me the keys.

A bright green
Mercedes-AMG GT63 S
E Performance at a car
show.

24

2025 MERCEDES-BENZ VISION ONE-ELEVEN

I'll finish my Dream-On Two Dozen with the Vision One-Eleven, a *Beam me up Scotty,* concept supercar from Planet Zog. Powered by four YASA axial-flux motors each generating 480 horsepower. And that adds up to a staggering 1920 horsepower. The One-Eleven was debuted at the 2023 IAA Munich Motor Show and is, according to Mercedes' Chief Design Officer, Gorden Wagener, not into retro-copying, even though those gullwings do recall this C111 prototype with its Wankel engine, seen here as the star of the 1969 Frankfurt Motor Show.

No. Herr Wagener maintains that the Vision One-Eleven is a design and tech showcase indicating where Mercedes luxury EVs will boldly go. Therein lies the spirit of Mercedes.

I'd really like to get behind the wheel of a One-Eleven, but I'd first be torn about which cabin version to choose. There are two — *Race Mode* with an upright driver-oriented set up and a compact steering wheel, and *Lounge Mode* with the seats laid flat into a continuous sculpture with the steering wheel designed to retract or not used at all because the car will be driving itself.

I know which one I would choose.

Above: A gold gullwing Vision One-Eleven on show at the IAA Mobility motor show.
Above right: The Vision One-Eleven from a different angle.
Opposite: An experimental Mercedes in 1969 from the C111 series.

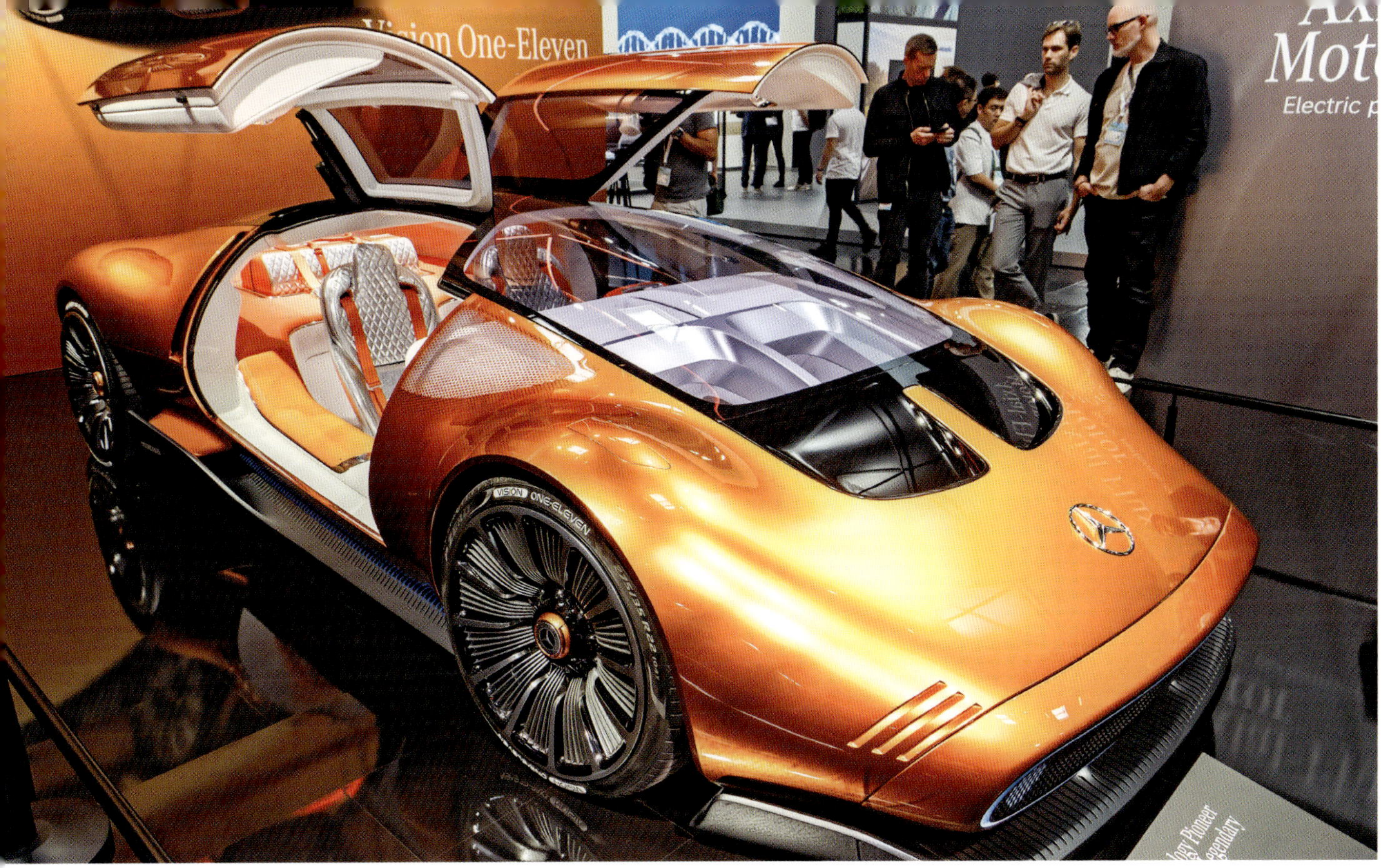
Vision One-Eleven
VISION ONE-ELEVEN

BOSCH
für die Zukunft des Automobils ist gesorgt

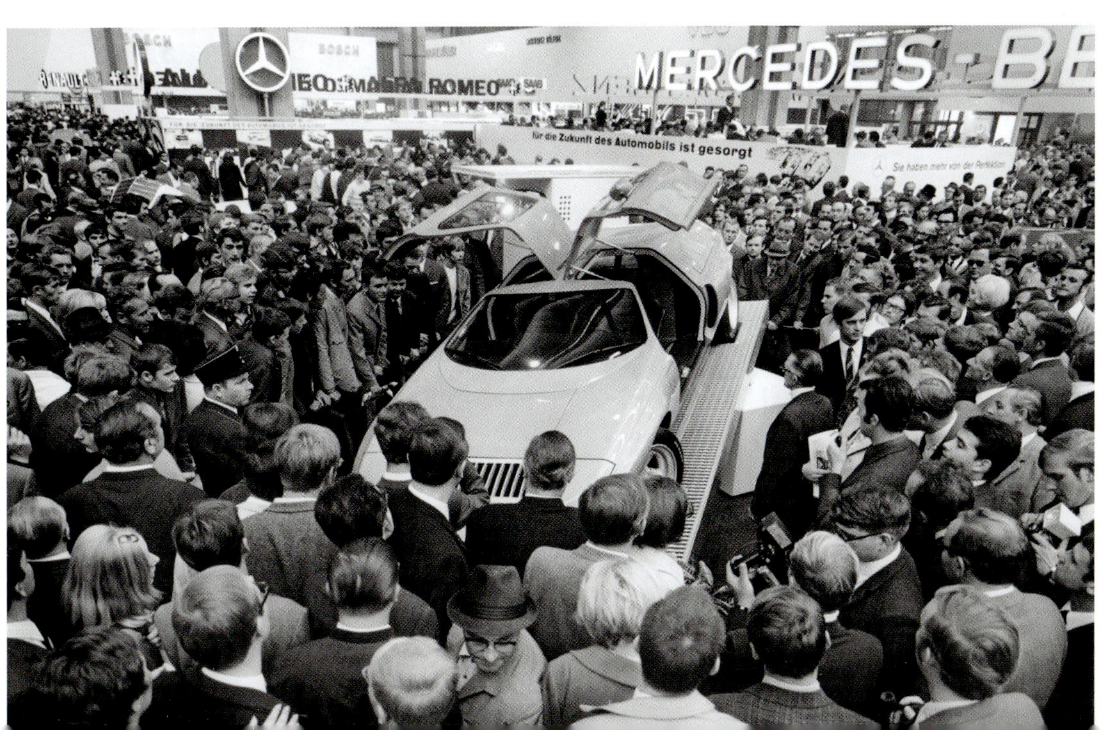

25

THE MERCEDES IMAGE

Who do you think of when it comes to the sort of person who drives a Mercedes today? Rich? Boss-man? Old? Male? Certainly there was a strong whiff of that in the past.

Today a Mercedes may still scream prestige and quality, but not sexism and snobbery.

Here a woman drives an SL500. She glances in the rear-view mirror. Car and driver are chill. Because they are both of today.

26

THAT LOGO

Is there any abstract logo in the car world as famous as that three-pointed star? Eat your heart out all you other car-makers.

It seems Gottlieb Daimler may have first used Mercedes' iconic logo on a postcard to his wife in 1872. He drew a three-pointed star over a picture of their home. On it he wrote:

One day this star will shine over my own factories to symbolize prosperity.

Daimler died in 1900 but his star lived on, for his design was remembered by his sons, Paul and Adolf. In 1909 it was registered by DMG, later explained as standing for Land (cars and trucks), Sea (boats and marine engines) and Air (airships and aircraft engines).

In 1926 when DMG and Benz & Cie merged, a laurel wreath was added to encircle the Mercedes and Benz names. Except it remained subordinate to the simple three-pointed star.

What should the simple star stand for today? Global Reach? Luxury? Precision? Except it's so famous, it doesn't need to stand for anything other than itself. Not unlike a statue which is more famous than its subject.

Here is a *before* on a 22 40HP, and two *afters*, a 36/220 Tourer and a 350 Mannheim. And, to make my point, Michelangelo's *David*.

Above: Michelangelo's statue *David*, Italy.
Opposite above: A Mercedes before the iconic logo was added to the front.
Opposite below: Two examples of the logo added to the front of the cars; a 36/220 Tourer (left) and a 350 Mannheim (right).

27

SOME MERCEDES DESIGNERS

There seem to be two approaches to designing a car. You can either start with designing the engineering first, just as Herren Benz, Daimler and Maybach did, and get around to designing the bodywork and interior afterwards, the approach Detroit would take to the extreme in the 1950s and 60s. Cars there were engineered purely as a mechanical platform which was then passed to brilliant stylists such as Harley Earl and Virgin Exner, who would add more and more chrome and change the fins for the next model year.

The other approach is *form follows function* – the Bauhaus way, that famous pre-war German design college which Hitler shut down for dictating the spirit of 20th century modernism. They proclaimed that aesthetics and engineering are simultaneous so that the result was an object whose beauty was inseparable from its purpose.

Today we see this harmony in aircraft design. We did see it in a few car brands such as SAAB, which wasn't surprising, as that now sadly defunct company was the child of an aircraft manufacturer. Today's equivalent would be Tesla followed by lots of non-legacy EV car

manufacturers, most of whose beginnings lay in designing attractive electronics. The result can be magnetic minimalism or shivery sterility — that's up to the eye of the beholder — but whichever it is, that design philosophy still has Bauhaus written all over it.

So where does this leave Mercedes-Benz? Well, as we've seen, the inventors of the world's first motorcars were engineers and engineering has been the driving force ever since.

Wilhelm Maybach may have seen elegance in engineering, but it took Hermann Ahrens, the Head of Special Vehicle Design at Mercedes' legendary Sindelfingen plant in the 1930s, to blend luxury with performance and flamboyant elegance. Sindelfingen, first set up in 1915 to produce aircraft for Daimler, would, under Ahrens, go on to concentrate on high-end coach-built models such as the 500K and 540K Spezial Roadsters.

From the 1950s to the 1960s, under Friedrich Geiger, automotive design became a defined discipline and not just a branch of engineering with bolt-on style. This was the age of the Mercedes industrial designer.

Opposite: Wilhelm Maybach.
Above: Hermann Ahrens.

Geiger appointed Paul Bracq as head of his Advanced Design Studio. It was a bold decision. Bracq, a Frenchman, had been undertaking National Service in the French Army in 1950s Germany, but beforehand had trained at Paris' prestigious Art & Design school, the École Boulle. Bracq would go on to design the elegant W111 and W112 Coupés and Cabriolets, the W100 Großer 600 limo and his most iconic car, the W113 'Pagoda' SL. Geiger's tenure was perhaps the most bold and resonant when it comes to turning out Mercedes classics. For example, Sindelfingen also designed such cars as the extraordinary 1954 300 SL 'Gullwing'.

From 1975 to 1999, Bruno Sacco was at the helm. We were now into the Bauhaus world of *Timeless Modernism*, that classic understatedness where cars are designed to never look dated. This was also the heyday of *horizontal homogeneity* as they called it, or to use plain English, you could see the family resemblance, whether the car was a W123-W126 or a W140 S-Class, a W124 E-Class, a R129 SL or a 190 E-Class. You could also see that, whichever model you chose, a Mercedes was not just horizontally homogenous, it was also hewn from granite and would go on forever.

Since 2008, Gorden Wagener has been Chief Design Officer. Enter
the world of design and hi-tech, especially with the EQ electric models.
Sensual Purity, they call it, or sometimes *Tech-Emotional Art*.

So where would I place the Mercedes-Benz marque on the Philosophy
of Automobile Design map? Engineering-led? Aesthetics-led? A
combination of the two? The answer is Mercedes-Benz has explored
the lot, simply because it has been around longer than any other car
manufacturer in the world. And a good thing too.

Nowe Marco Polo Horizon
Klasy V

28

MPV MERCEDES

I know. I know. Multi-Purpose Vehicle. Not terribly fashionable today. But bloody useful, especially when you have a large brood and couldn't care less about image — or price. Except there are some that are instant classics, such as this cool Marco Polo. It is not only all-singing and dancing, but as its name implies, is raring to go anywhere.

Can a Mercedes Marco Polo ever become as cool as a classic Volkswagen van, here owned by one of my daughters? Silly question. Except you won't have this happen to you.

29

OFF-ROAD MERCEDES

When it comes to toughness with class, there is only one way to go – a Mercedes G-Wagen. This AMG G63 fits the bill, because not only will it soldier on forever, conquering mountains, streams, deserts, tundra, you name it, but will do so in sheer style. Except it won't go to any of those places. And you will not know whether it can soldier on forever, or even care, because you will change it as soon as a newer model comes out. Maybe sooner.

In London, they are called *Chelsea Tractors*. Actually, this one is next door in Kensington, although it could reach Chelsea with ease.

This Mercedes Geländewagen has managed to reach Dubai, as has its Lamborghini Aventador companion.

Above: A Lamborghini Aventador and a Mercedes G-Wagen matching in yellow. Opposite: A black Mercedes AMG G63 in Kensington, London.

FJERÅ
Väst...

30

WACKY MERCEDES

Sometimes people do funny things, (by which I mean odd, amusing
or often both), to the world's most famous marque. At the Emirates
National Auto Museum, you can see a Merc fully set up to tackle the
largest sand dunes in the world. Presumably.

Or, how about a carefully curated wreck, such as this one in
Argentina? Don't cry.

31

RACING MERCEDES

Mercedes began racing and rallying in 1894 when a Daimler-powered car won the Paris-Rouen race. Then there was that 35 PS which blasted aside all competition.

In the 1930s, Mercedes' fielded their iconic *Silver Arrow* cars, the W25, W125 and W154. These dominated inter-war Grands Prix. Before 1934, Germany's racing colour was white but it was then changed to silver, supposedly because when the cars were stripped of paint, weight was saved. Here is a W125 supercharged straight eight producing up to 640hp. Astonishing for 1937.

The early 1950s saw the classic W196R, which will forever be associated with its driver and five times F1 winner, Juan Manuel Fangio.

Above: Argentine racing car driver Juan Manuel Fangio.
Opposite: A silver 1937 W125 Grand Prix racing Mercedes on show in the Musée National de l'Automobile.

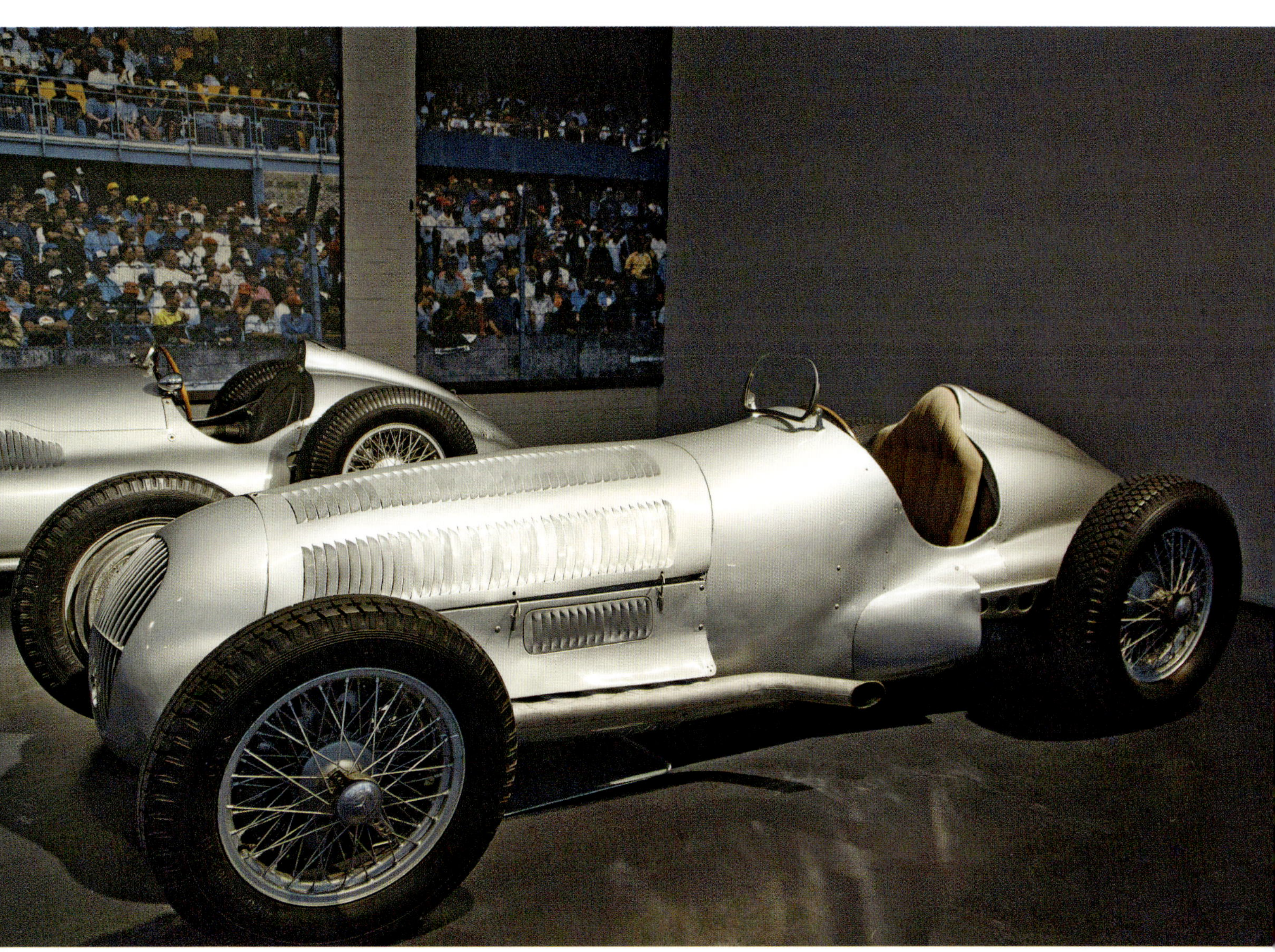

Then there was the 300 SLR which we've already seen, in which Stirling Moss won the Mille Miglia in record time. This, of course, was also the model that in 1955 killed 84 people at Le Mans, resulting in Mercedes' withdrawal from motor racing for the next 30 years.

In 1989 Mercedes, which since 1985 had partnered with Sauber, the Swiss motorsport engineering company in Group C endurance racing, won Le Mans in their 5 litre twin turbo-charged Sauber-Mercedes C9. It was a magnificent comeback. Here are the three entered cars just after winning first, second and fifth place, surrounded by adoring fans and the press.

The first, second and fifth placing Sauber-Mercedes C9S at Le Mans in 1989.

And so we come to what is perhaps the most dominant F1 car ever. Drive forward the scorching Mercedes-AMG W11 EQ Performance, the car in which Sir Lewis Hamilton won his 7th title. Here is Sir Lewis' 2022 F1 Championship-winning car. Nuff said.

Or maybe not. Because just sometimes, do *you* envy racing drivers? What about your very own Mercedes AMG ONE. She is street legal, yet F1, she will deliver 1000hp, max out at 217mph (350kph) and offer you sub-6.30 Nürburgring laps. After a few lessons of course.

Above: Sir Lewis Hamilton's 2022 F1-winning Mercedes-AMG W11 EQ.
Opposite: A blue AMG One on show in a Mercedes-Benz showroom in Monaco.

Here is one in a Monaco showroom – where else? – waiting for collection. Except there are only 275 in the world and each will set you back $2.7 million. That's if you can get one new. The good news is that if you do, you could sell it for up to $5.4 million on the open market. Fast car. Fast buck.

32

MILITARY MERCEDES

It's a bit 'do we need to go there?' when this subject comes up. After all, there are plenty of books for military buffs and re-enactors showing old pics of Rommel and Co with their Mercedes military cars – sitting in them, standing in them, saluting in them, or merely getting in and out of them.

We'll stay with today. Here is a Mercedes LAPV (Light Armoured Patrol Vehicle) 6.2 Enok. Based on the G-Class (as if you hadn't guessed), this LAPV Enok is used mainly by the *Kommando Spezialkräfte* or German Special Forces Command and is designed for reconnaissance, patrol, VIP protection and command roles. It is covered in Rheinmet armour, including the important floor pan.

All this provides heavy-duty blast protection. Yet given its weight of 4.5-5.4 tonnes, Enok can manage up to 80mph (130kph) on the road thanks to its 250hp 3 litre V6 Turbo Diesel. Amazing.

By the way, the English designation LAPV is thanks to NATO lingo standardization. Which of course means American. Except Enok is German for a type of wildcat or lynx, known to be fast, light and survivable.

33

POLICE MERCEDES

In the past, police forces favoured Mercedes cars as they were fast, reliable and authoritative. Mercedes meant business. They looked the part. And still do. Here is a 1950s Mercedes ad aimed at those holding the coppers of the world's purse strings.

Today additional considerations, especially green ones, have come into play. Here in 2019 is Hamburg's first fuel cell-powered police car being handed over by Mercedes-Benz to Hamburg Police. Left to right, police chief, Hartmut Dudde Police Commissioner, Ralf Meyer and Mercedes-Benz Head of Sales, Matthias Kallis.

I wasn't planning to feature Mercedes' foray into Smart, but when I saw this photo I thought why not? After all, we've all seen movies about New York's Finest, and we expect big cars for big cops. Not any more. Here is NYPD's Mini.

Above: Hamburg's first fuel cell-powered radio patrol car.
Opposite above: Vintage Mercedes ad targeting the police.
Opposite below: An NYPD Mercedes Smart car.

MERCEDES-BENZ

UA
BH 0063 HO
Mercedes-Benz Автомобільний Дім Україна ☎ 044 201 60 00
248-8-248
248-8-248

34

MERCEDES FROM THE FRONT

An E63 AMG in camouflage. With most lesser marques, disguise is easy. With a Merc, no way.

A camouflaged
Mercedes Benz E 63
AMG parked in Kiev.

35

MERCEDES FROM THE REAR

It has to be admitted that some people don't like the Mercedes marque, especially when it passes them. So when one is stationary, there is a dissing opportunity. But that's less about the car and more about the sort of people who drive them. Here is the rear of a gorgeous 1969 280 SL in Alsace, France.

Gardez les yeux sur la route, monsieur! Jaloux? Moi?

Above: Two for the road, naughtly diverted from driving a 280SL. Opposite: Some graffiti in the dirt on the back of a white Bluetech Mercedes.

Mercedes-Benz of Bury St Edmunds IP32 6NH
www.mercedes-benzofburystedmunds.co.uk
PURE FILTH

36

MERCEDES FROM THE SIDE

The only word to describe a Merc when viewed from the side is *sleek*.

Hold on — what about those van Mercs, such as this all-electric 2025 EQV 300?

Well yes, except when you climb into the driving seat of this van-Merc — indeed any Merc — you just don't think like that. You think of an S-Class, such as this in an underground parking lot.

And when you climb into the driving seat of this S-Class, you think you're in something like a Mercedes T80 from the 1930s. Right?

Whichever Mercedes you are at the wheel of and whatever it looks like, *a Merc feels sleek*.

Opposite above: A fully electric EQV300 Mercedes-Benz van
Opposite middle: A side view of the Mercedes S-Class in a parking lot.
Opposite below: The Mercedes T80 on display at the Mercedes-Benz museum.

MERCEDES FROM THE TOP

Mercedes cars can look great from above, especially when they are drop-heads. Here, from different eras, are a red SL 500 (see overleaf on left), a grey AMG and a classic silver 300 SL Gullwing (see overleaf on right).

Actually we don't often study cars from above, especially our C-Class estate. Except when we keep sticking our head out of a window to see whether there is a traffic warden hovering nearby.

Opposite: A red SL 500
from above.
Right: A silver 300 SL
Gullwing from above.

4MATIC
EQC 400 4MATIC

38

INSIDE A MERCEDES

Cars are designed so we cannot see what is actually going on inside. Rather like us really.

Here we see the inside and the outside of an EQC. Apart from the wheels, can you match one to the other? Me neither. But what I can do, and it's the reason I chose this model, is figure out the inside story of the EQC. As will you.

It was built in Bremen and China, with the Chinese car manufacturer BAIC. Yet it was only sold from 2019 to 2023, a blink of an eye for a new model.

You may well ask why — because this was Mercedes' first all-electric car. This should have socked it to them. The answer is that in a panic to get into the game ASAP, Mercedes cut a few corners. And that is not a very Mercedes thing to do.

A shiny electric Mercedes EQC 400 4Matic 300kW at the Mondial Paris Motor Show.

With Chinese 'help and advice', Mercedes had adapted their internal combustion-engine GLC model. And that meant some key drawbacks, such as a short battery range and a high price.

So what should have been a show-stopper, bombed. Because in those few short years, the EQC found itself up against a flood of brilliantly designed-from-scratch and less expensive electric cars. From China mostly. Including BAIC. Ouch.

The internal systems of the electric Mercedes EQC 400 4Matic 300 kW SUV.

39

MERCEDES COCKPITS

Why do the cockpits of Mercedes classic cars always look so
marvellous? Just feast your eyes on these – a 300 SL, 280 SE, 280SL
and 170 Coupé. Is there much competition? I don't think so.

Above and opposite:
Various Mercedes-Benz
interiors.

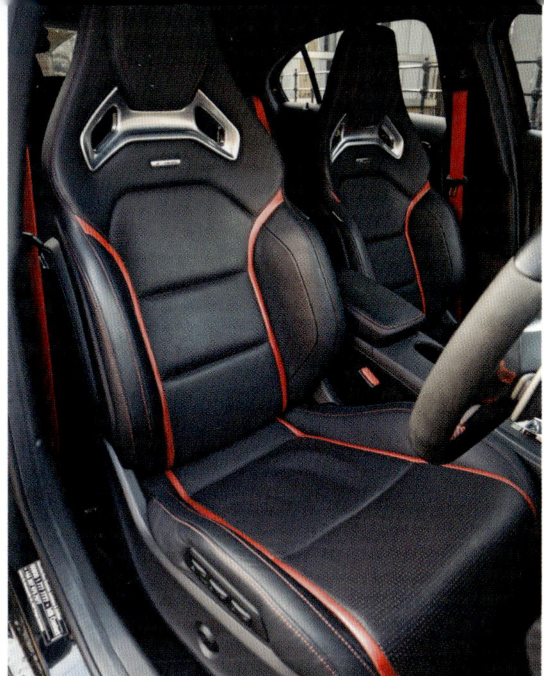

40

MERCEDES SEATS

Mercedes car seats have always been generous on size and padding. My 280 SL is the only car I've ever owned that gives full support behind my knees.

This 2014 A45 AMG gives great bottom and thigh comfort, as does this 1971 220 SE Coupé.

However, if you are into the bling thing, how about this AG Excalibur based on a CL 500 platform? This car comes with Swarovski crystal buttons. Apparently the seats are at least as comfortable as those in a regular Mercedes.

AG stands for Audronis Gestautas, an exclusive endeavour in Lithuania, which specializes in flamboyant coupés for those who like that sort of thing and can afford their eye-watering price tags.

41

MERCEDES ROAD WHEELS

There are at least six wheels on a Mercedes automobile – four on the road, one in the driver's hands and the wheel that says it all – that logo.

It wasn't always this way. The three-pointed star wasn't set in a roundel back in the day. This 1920s model (opposite) having its wheels pumped up has had to go without. But when it came to be, it was pretty obvious where it had to go.

42

A FEW MERCEDES INVENTIONS

We all know that Karl Benz introduced the first automobile in 1886, the *Patent Motorwagen*, designed to be driven on public roads and powered by an internal combustion engine. But in 1901 the 35 PS then introduced the first pressed-steel dropped chassis which lowered the centre of gravity. And while they were at it that year, the company introduced the honeycomb radiator for engine heat control. Cool or what?

Then 1931 said hello to the first car with four-wheel independent suspension, the 170, and in 1936 the first diesel passenger car, the 260 D.

After WWII, the name of the game was safety first. So, in 1959, Mercedes introduced the Crumple Zone on the W111 Fintail, designed by that doyen of automobile engineers, Bela Barényi.

In 1978 it was ABS on the W116 S-Class, in 1981 the first airbags in Europe on the W126 S-Class, in 1986 the first traction control to prevent wheel spin on all high-end Mercedes and in 1995 the first electronic stability programme (ESP) on the W140 S-Class and the R129 SL.

I could go on but I think you get the picture of a relentless R & D programme at Mercedes.

Mercedes has also taken systems that others introduced but Mercedes perfected, such as seatbelt pre-tensioners, night vision assist and, my favourite, stereo cameras in 2013 to scan and adjust the suspension to road irregularities. They called it *Magic Body Control*. We would all like that.

Workers pose for a photo at the Benz & Cie. factory at Mannheim.

Many have been not only great inventions for safety, but also fun for drivers too, such as in 2018 which saw the first car with an AI voice-command infotainment system, *Hey Mercedes*.

Talking *Hey Mercedes*, here is a picture to show that while there have always been stars at the company (think Bela with his crumple zones), perfecting clever designs has always required a team effort.

In fact, it's touching to see those first involved in creating what would become the most famous car brand in the world lined up for a group picture.

Above: The Benz patent motor car Model 1, 1886. Opposite: The Daimler 2-cylinder engine.

43

MERCEDES ENGINES

Karl Benz did not build the first internal combustion engine. That honour goes to Étienne Lenoir who made a crude ICE in 1860. In 1876, Nicolaus Otto made a brilliant four-stroke engine. But what Karl then did in 1885 was to perfect Nicolaus' design, introducing throttle control, water-cooling, a clutch and gear system. That meant the creation of what we would recognize today as the first functioning car in the world.

Very hot on the heels of Karl's three-wheeled *Benz Patent-Motorwagen* (into which he had fitted this engine) was Daimler & Maybach. In 1886, the four-wheeler into which they inserted a more powerful and versatile engine – lighter, faster-revving and using petrol – was called the *Grandfather Clock* because it looked like the inside of one.

Mercedes has been at the forefront of engine technology, from the 1901 35 PS 5.9L inline 4, through to the 1937 5.6 litre super-charged V8 which drove those amazing *Silver Arrows*, and on to the post-war 300 SL engine with mechanical fuel injection, inspired by aviation.

The 1960s to 80s saw those wonderful V8s - from the 6.3 versions (W100, W109) with their air suspension to the 6.9 (M100) with its dry sump lubrication - all wafting along their top of the range cars. Like the cars themselves, these engines were built to last forever.

Various Mercedes-Benz engines from over the years.

The 1990s saw the first V12s, super-refined, and fitted to the S600, SL600 and the CLK GTR and from 2002 to 2020 the V12 Biturbo – massive torque and 621 horsepower which powered the S65 AMG and the Maybach cars.

By 2015, Mercedes was getting an insane 730 horsepower out of a 4 litre V8 Biturbo – the M178 engine.

Yet it is the M139 of 2019 to the present that is in many ways the most impressive, not least because it offers 421 horsepower out of a 2 litre, 4 cylinder turbocharged unit. This engine, fitted to the AMG A45 S and variants, is the world's most powerful production four-pot. Hand-assembled, it is perhaps the final frontier of what the internal combustion engine can achieve in today's emissions-conscious world.

Which in the same year brings us to a denuded all-electric EQC 400 4Matic EQ. Its engine produces 300kW.

44

CRASH MERCEDES

Mercedes has one of the best reputations in the world for designing and building safe cars. Think of the crumple zones they invented.

These journalists have been invited along by Mercedes to see how they work when they crash two electric cars at 35mph (56kph) – an EQS SUV and an EQA Crossover XSUV. After the test, both passenger cabins and the high-voltage battery packs were fully intact.

And here are two crash test dummies taking a look around Mercedes-Benz World at Brooklands, England. They were impressed in more ways than one.

Mercedes is aiming for none of its vehicles to be involved in any crash at all by 2050.

Above: Crash test dummies looking around Mercedes Benz World, Surrey.
Opposite: Some crash-tested Mercedes.

Jagdwagen Seiner Majestät des Kaisers Wilhelm II
geliefert von der

Daimler-Motoren-Gesellschaft
Stuttgart-Untertürkheim.

45

MERCEDES ADS

When it comes to drawing attention to itself, Mercedes has always aimed high. In 1907 that meant the Emperor of Germany, no less. This advertisement recommends you too should have a hunting car, just like Kaiser Bill himself.

After World War I, but before Hitler arrived, along came the Weimar Republic and the Flapper Age. Mercedes now meant not just the money but the fun too. Here are Willy Fritsch and Lilian Harvey – Germany's Fred Astaire and Ginger Rogers – living it up around 1929.

Coupe d'Etat

For over half a century, it has been the pleasure of men of state to drive or be driven in a Mercedes-Benz. Mercedes-Benz now offers its newest car, a veritable coupe of state, to the discriminating few who can afford to be seen in this, the finest of machines. It is the new 220 SE coupe with a fuel injection engine, optional power steering and a choice of automatic or four-speed transmission. Its interior is completely hand-fitted with elegant leather and wood embellishments and represents the best of the coachmaker's art. There is no similar car in the world. It combines sportslike performance with the dignity of diplomacy. Further, it carries its silver three-pointed star in the restful silence of complete discretion. That, of course, is entirely in keeping with the seventy-five-year-old tradition of Mercedes-Benz.

Mercedes-Benz Sales, Inc., South Bend, Indiana (*A Subsidiary of Studebaker-Packard Corporation*)

After World War II, Mercedes focused on America. In 1962 this ad unashamedly presses the exclusivity button. Even if you cannot afford this splendid 220 SE Coupé, the message is that any Mercedes is going to put you up there where you should belong.

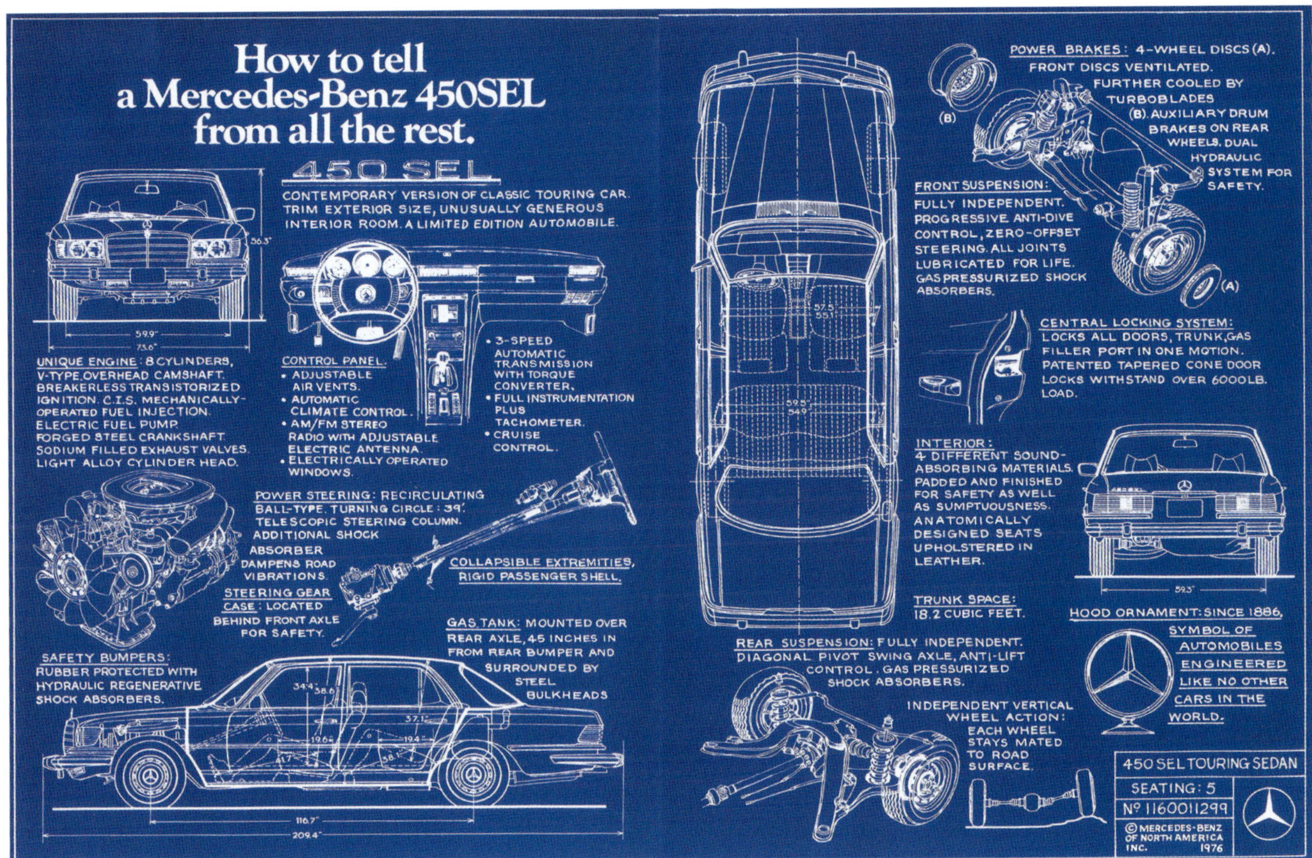

By 1976, safety was becoming all the rage in the US, and who better to provide it than Mercedes-Benz. This ad cleverly uses a blueprint to emphasize how scientific the company is in its approach. Which, of course was true. *How to tell a Mercedes-Benz from all the rest*, may have ostensibly been aimed at you, but you knew subconsciously, that when you bought a Mercedes, others could then tell you from all the rest. Snobbery and Safety as bedfellows. Genius.

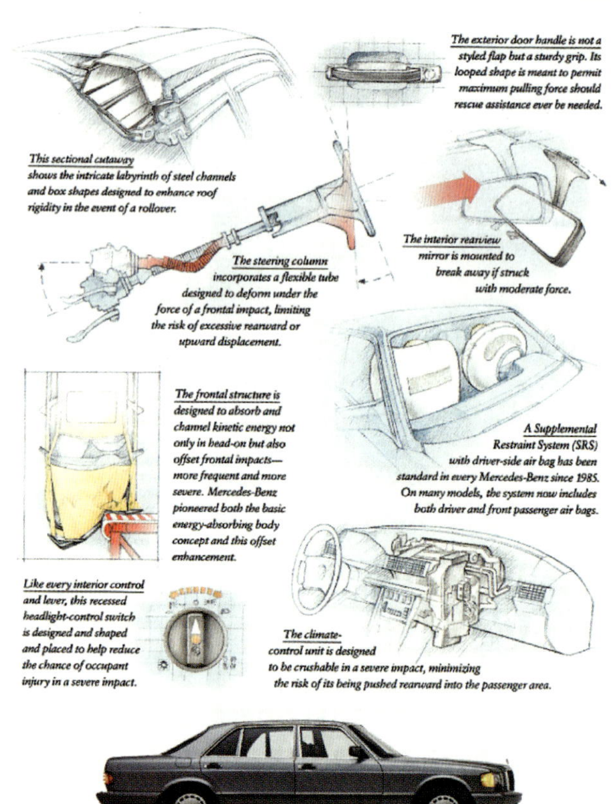

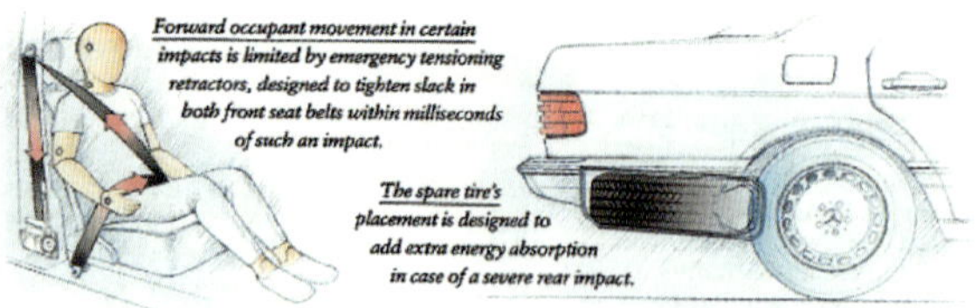

A crash course in Mercedes-Benz

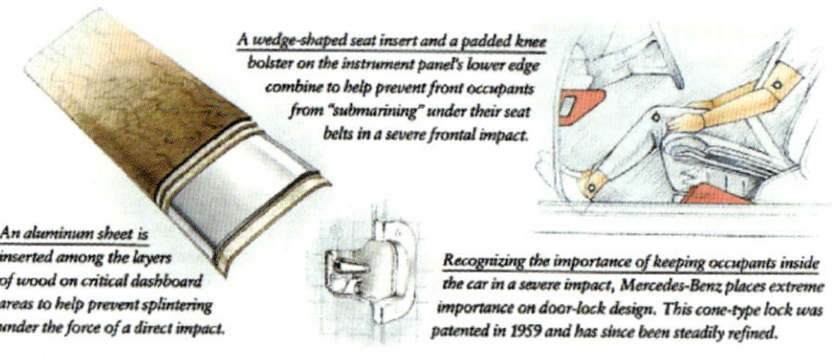

The most effective single safety element is still the seat belt. So please, buckle up—even if you drive a Mercedes-Benz. For more information about Mercedes-Benz safety, call 1-800-243-9292 or visit your authorized Mercedes-Benz dealer. Some of the safety features depicted vary from model to model.

ENGINEERED LIKE NO OTHER CAR IN THE WORLD

By the 1980s, safety was mainstream and Mercedes had positioned itself as King of Safety. This ad assumes you know quite a lot about automobile design. It displays Mercedes' famous strapline – *Engineered like no other car in the world*. Topped with that obligatory three-pointed star.

In 2009 this huge billboard appeared in the centre of Berlin. People still talk about it. Spectacle was the thing. But ubiquitous social media has since hit the ad world of the billboard. Time moves on. Certainly in the fashion business.

46

MERCEDES IN CHINA

In 2013 China became Mercedes' largest single national market, surpassing the US and Germany itself.

The first cars, imported in 1986, were limited to Chinese government use and, of course, foreign VIPs, but it wasn't until 2005 that Mercedes started to expand big-time through that joint venture with Beijing Automotive Industry Holding (BAIC), as I've mentioned before. Mercedes and BAIC set up BBAC, the Beijing Benz Automotive Co. Ltd, and started by building C- and E-Class cars.

In 2015, longer-wheelbase sedans were called for by the Chinese market, (no, I don't know why), which was so successful that by 2022 the largest Mercedes factory in the world was in China.

Since then, the name of the game has been electric, with the focus on digital retail, connectivity and autonomous driving, which is what Chinese punters now expect. Unsurprisingly, the challenge for Mercedes is the rapid growth of home grown competition who are focused on exactly the same.

So is Mercedes a German company or a Chinese one? Well, BAIC holds 9.98 per cent of voting rights, while Chinese billionaire, Li Shufu of Geely, which incidentally owns Volvo and Polestar, holds 9.69 per cent of Mercedes-Benz Group AG. So nearly 20 per cent of Mercedes-Benz is currently Chinese-owned.

There are sleek Mercedes-Benz dealerships all over China such as this one in Yichun. Speaking of the Chinese penchant for stretched wheelbases, here in Beijing is a stretch carrying North Korean leader Kim Jong Un on his way to Beijing Railway Station and then home.

Opposite above: A modern Mercedes dealership in China.
Opposite below: A stretch Mercedes limo takes Kim Jong Un to his destination.

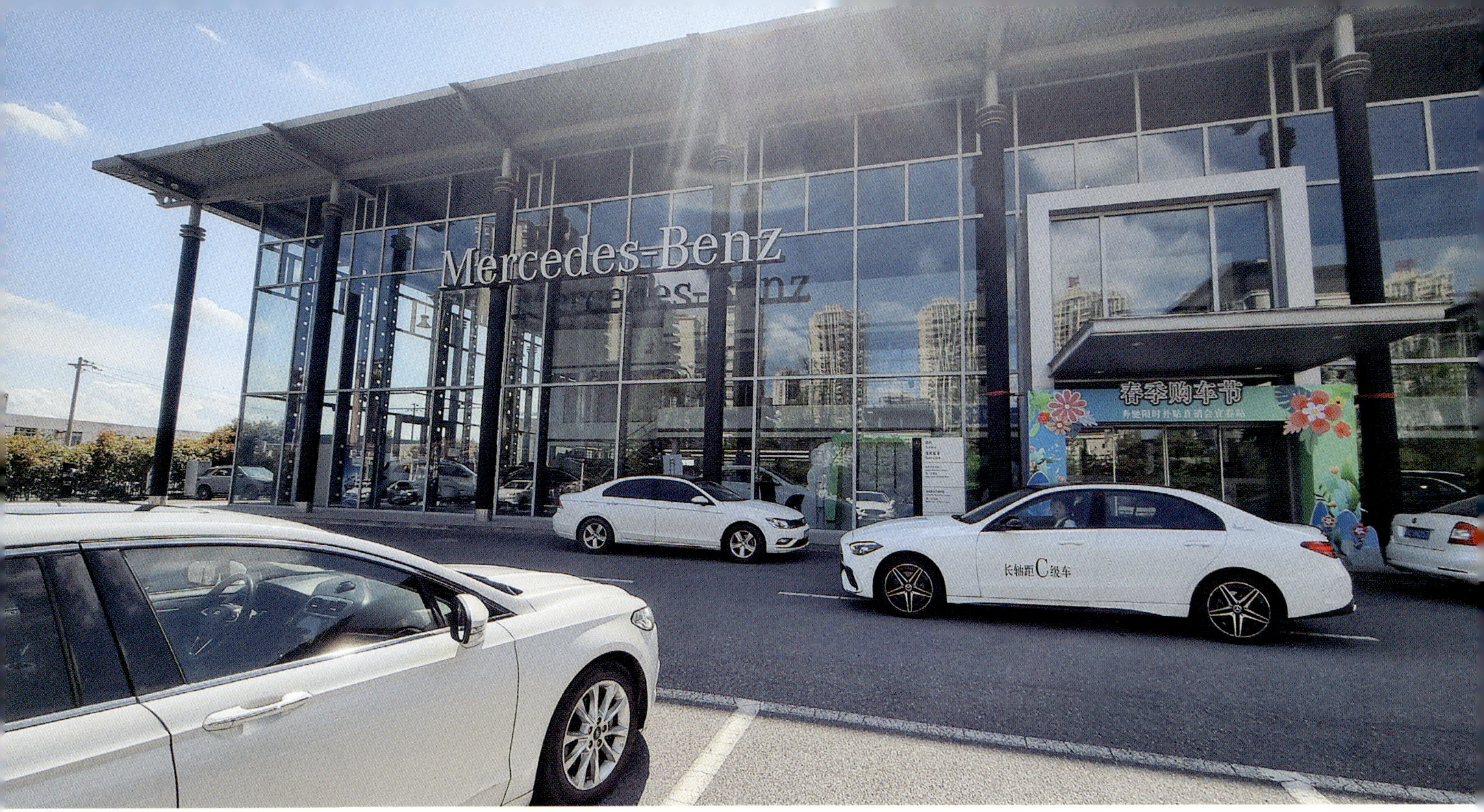
Mercedes-Benz
春季购车节
长轴距C级车

此处禁止停放任何车辆

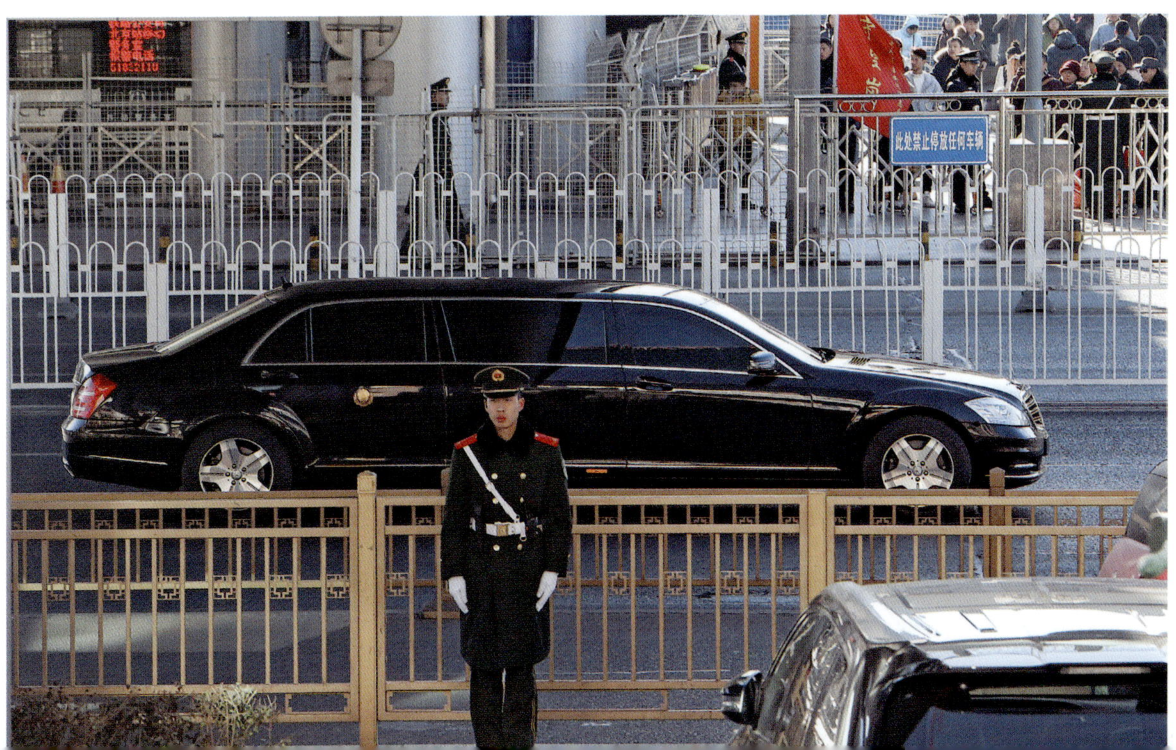

The Sindelfingen factory
in Germany.

47

MERCEDES AROUND THE WORLD

Mercedes' largest car plant may be in Beijing, but their most cutting edge is still at Sindelfingen near Stuttgart – the headquarters of Mercedes design, research and development, as it has been for almost a century. Today it is also the main manufacturing centre for Mercedes' flagship luxury sedans and electric cars.

Other automobile plants in Germany include Bremen, the largest Mercedes manufacturer in Europe, which focuses on SUVs and compacts and Rastatt, which also makes compacts as well as entry-level electric cars.

At Uusikaupunki, Finland, Mercedes uses the well-respected contract car manufacturer Valmet Automotive for overflow production.

In North America, Mercedes' main plant is at Tuscaloosa, Alabama producing, unsurprisingly, SUVs (both internal combustion and electric) for the US and Canadian markets but also for worldwide export.

Mercedesstraße

East London, South Africa produces C-Class cars for global export as well as the South African market.

Mercedes shares a plant with Nissan at Aguascalientes, Mexico, making compact cars for the Central and North American markets.

This bird's-eye-view photograph from 2024 shows Sindelfingen's Factory 56, Mercedes-Benz's state-of-the-art electric car plant which opened in 2020. Mercedes' Research & Development and MTC (Mercedes Technology Centre) stands behind. Beyond that is the medieval Aldstadt of Sindelfingen, which is well worth a visit. Beyond the medieval town and also well worth a visit, is the Schönbuch Nature Park with its beguiling woodlands and deer. It provides a natural green belt between Sindelfingen and Stuttgart, which is just over the horizon. You may see some high-rises peeping up.

48

MERCEDES HQ

Stuttgart, capital of the German state of Baden-Württemberg, is the global headquarters of three world-famous German brands – Bosch, Porsche and Mercedes.

When Daimler and Benz joined forces in 1926, the company name they agreed on was, quite understandably, Daimler-Benz AG, (*Aktiengesellschaft*, a company limited by shares) which represented everything the company made – cars, vans, trucks or buses, etc.

Daimler-Benz AG lasted until 1998, when it was changed to DaimlerChrysler AG, thanks to that unwise marriage. In 2007 when the marriage had finally fallen apart, it became simply Daimler AG, but that still meant cars, vans, trucks and buses, etc.

But in 2021 a major split was announced. The Daimler name was dropped in favour of the Mercedes name, which everyone recognized – certainly in China – so on 1 February 2022 the *Aktiengesellschaft* became Mercedes-Benz Group AG. The cars were finally acknowledged as being in first place.

You may ask why Herr Benz kept his name on the masthead, while the company's equal founders, Herren Daimler and Maybach were dumped. That seems a bit unfair. Why not just Mercedes Group AG?

Does any of this matter? Not really. Because that three-pointed star says all that needs to be said. What other *Aktiengesellschaften* is so lucky?

Daimler-Konzernzentrale
Mercedes-Benz Werk Untertürkheim

49

MERCEDES AND MAYBACH MUSEUMS

As you approach the Mercedes-Benz Museum in Stuttgart, which is next to their headquarters, you will see a life-size bronze composition of a figure standing next to a racing car. It is by the Catalan sculptor, Joaquim Ros i Sabate and it depicts Juan Manuel Fangio with his iconic Mercedes-Benz W196 R.

Having this statue at the entrance to the museum tells you a lot about Mercedes-Benz. History and legacy are important, which is why they have given pole position to the world's most famous racing driver and the car he drove for them.

Inside the museum is a stunning array of Mercedes cars from their very beginnings to the present day. If only we had space to show more pictures, but better still, visit yourself.

DESIGN
INSPIRATION

A display of concept cars in the Mercedes museum.

Should you do so, and you still want more, why not drive down to *Neumarkt in der Oberpfalz* and visit the fascinating Maybach Museum. It will take you about two and a half hours from Stuttgart. The museum was founded by Helmut Hofmann in 2009 and is the only one in the world devoted to Maybachs. *www.automuseum-maybach.de*

But should you fancy a three-day round trip, you could carry on to Friedrichshafen, home of Zeppelin, Dornier Aviation and Maybach. There you will see the former Maybach factory. And being on Lake Constance, it's a beautiful place to stay overnight.

Opposite and above:
Cars on display in the
Maybach museum.

50

FINAL THOUGHTS

Why do I love Mercedes? Well, once upon a time, when I was a young lecturer at a London university, I decided to start my own course teaching graduates to teach. I had noticed that while some of my fellow lecturers were experts in their subjects, they didn't seem so good at communicating it to their students. That wasn't surprising as they had never been taught to teach, whereas I had.

A couple of years later, a colleague, who was lecturing on another course, said:

'You are very lucky teaching those students of yours, Vaughan!'

'Oh yes? Why's that?'

'Because they all have Mercedes minds.'

I decided I then needed the car to go with the students. So I bought the one I'd always wanted – a 1969 280 SL. And then, when I drove it, I realized that it must have been Mercedes minds that, from the very beginning, had given Mercedes-Benz its spirit. And still did.

No, I wasn't about to start teaching my students how to design cars. Not that I could. But here are some of my students from long, long ago with my beautiful Mercedes.

Mind and spirit meeting together. That's Mercedes-Benz.

The author (sitting in front) with a class of his students and his Mercedes 280 SL.

ABOUT THE AUTHOR

Vaughan Grylls is an artist and writer. He lives in London and East Kent and has been a Mercedes enthusiast since 1982 when he bought his classic 1969 280 SL pagoda. Some years later, the arrival of a family meant a sensible C-Class was called for. His children have now grown up and left home so Vaughan is very relieved to once more not be sensible.

ACKNOWLEDGEMENTS

This book would not have been possible without the assistance of the Technical Team at the Mercedes-Benz Club UK (for more information go to https://mercedes-benz-club.co.uk/) for their valuable comments and advice on the technical aspects and history of Mercedes-Benz, Magda Simões-Brown at Batsford Books for her editorial skills and advice and Ferdy Carabott for resuscitating several ancient, yet key images.

First published in the
United Kingdom
in 2026 by
Batsford
43 Great Ormond Street
London
WC1N 3HZ

An imprint of B. T. Batsford Holdings
Limited

ISBN 978 1 83733 024 9

A CIP catalogue record for this book is
available from the British Library.

10 9 8 7 6 5 4 3 2 1

Reproduction by Mission Productions,
Hong Kong
Printed by Toppan Leefung Printing
International Ltd, China

This book can be ordered direct from the
publisher at www.batsfordbooks.com, or
try your local bookshop.

Distributed throughout the UK and Europe
by Abrams & Chronicle Books, 1st Floor,
22–24 Ely Place, London EC1N 6TE
and 57 rue Gaston Tessier, 75166 Paris,
France.

www.abramsandchronicle.co.uk
info@abramsandchronicle.co.uk

PICTURE CREDITS